Contents

Note on the Author and Editors

GEOFFREY CHAUCER, the son of a wine merchant in London, was born about 1343 or 1344. He was a voracious reader of Latin, French and Italian literature, and of works of science, philosophy and religion. Apart from *The Canterbury Tales* he wrote several long and distinguished poems – *The Book of the Duchess*, *The House of Fame*, *The Parliament of Fowls*, *Troilus and Criseyde* and *The Legend of Good Women*. He also made a prose translation of *The Consolation of Philosophy* by Boethius and of a treatise on the astrolabe. Yet the writing of poetry and prose was often a spare-time occupation for Chaucer, who was successively a member of the King's Household, a soldier, a diplomatic envoy to France and Italy, a high customs official, a justice of the peace, a member of parliament, and Clerk of the King's Works. From all these activities he gained the knowledge of men and women which made it possible for him to write *The Canterbury Tales*. Chaucer died at Westminster in 1400.

MALCOLM ANDREW has been Professor of English Language and Literature at the Queen's University of Belfast since 1985. His publications on medieval literature include an edition of *The Poems of the Pearl Manuscript* (with Ronald Waldron, 1978; 3rd ed. 1996), an annotated bibliography of writings on the *Gawain*-Poet (1979), a collection of essays on *The Canterbury Tales* (1991) and the Variorum edition of the *General Prologue* (with Charles Moorman and Daniel J. Ransom, 1993).

A. C. CAWLEY was Darnell Professor of English in the University of Queensland, 1959–65, and Professor of English Language and Medieval English Literature in the University of Leeds, 1965–79. His editions of *The Wakefield Pageants in the Towneley Cycle* and of *Everyman* were first published in 1958 and 1961, and *Chaucer's Mind and Art* in 1968.

Chronology of Chaucer's Life

Year	Life
*c.*1312–13	Birth of Chaucer's father, John Chaucer
*c.*1343–4	Birth of Chaucer, son of John and Agnes Chaucer, in London
1357	In service as a page in the household of Elizabeth, Countess of Ulster (wife of Lionel, Earl of Ulster, second son of Edward III)
1359–60	Service in the retinue of Lionel on campaign in France; ransomed after being captured at the siege of Reims

Chronology of his Times

Year	Literary and Historical Events
1313	Birth of Boccaccio
1321	Death of Dante, soon after the completion of the *Divina Commedia*
1327	Accession of Edward III, aged 14
1337–1453	The Hundred Years' War between England and France
1338	Completion of Boccaccio's *Il Filostrato* (main source of Chaucer's *Troilus and Criseyde*)
1341	Completion of Boccaccio's *Teseide delle Nozze d'Emilia* (main source of *The Knight's Tale*)
1346	English victory at the battle of Crécy
1348–9	About one third of the population of England dies in the Black Death
1350s	Beginnings of the revival of alliterative poetry in the West and North-West of England
1356	English victory at the battle of Poitiers; capture of King John of France, who lives at the English court, 1357–60
1360	Treaty of Brétigny brings peace between England and France until 1369
1361–7	Jean Froissart, the French chronicler and poet, present in the household of Queen Philippa (wife of Edward III)
1364	Death of King John of France; accession of Charles V

Year	Life
*c.*1365–66	Marries Philippa Roet, eldest daughter of the Flemish knight Sir Paon de Roet, and sister of Katherine (later Katherine Swynford)
1366	Death of Chaucer's father; his mother shortly remarries. Philippa Chaucer mentioned as a 'domicelle' of Queen Philippa, wife of Edward III
1367	In service as an esquire in the household of Edward III; granted an annuity for life by the King
*c.*1367	Birth of a son, Thomas
late 1360s	Translates part of the *Roman de la Rose*; possibly also writing poetry in French at this time
1368–9	Writes *The Book of the Duchess* on the death of Blanche, Duchess of Lancaster
1369	Serves in campaign of John of Gaunt in Northern France
1370	Travels to the Continent on the King's business
*c.*1372–7	Writes the poems later adapted as *The Second Nun's Tale* and *The Monk's Tale*
1372	Philippa Chaucer in service in the household of John of Gaunt
1372–3	Travels to Genoa (to establish an English port for Genoese trade) and to Florence (to negotiate a loan for the King)
1374	Granted a pitcher of wine daily by the King and an annuity of £10 by John of Gaunt. Appointed Controller of Customs for hides, skins, and wools in the port of London; leases a house above Aldgate

Year	Literary and Historical Events
mid 1360s	William Langland begins *Piers Plowman* (the 'A-text')
1367	January: birth of Richard of Bordeaux, later Richard II, second and only surviving son of Edward, the Black Prince (eldest son of Edward III) Battle of Najera, in which the Black Prince supports Pedro of Castile. The King addresses Parliament in English for the first time
1368	September: death of Blanche, Duchess of Lancaster, first wife of John of Gaunt (third son of Edward III)
1369	Assassination of Pedro of Castile. Renewal of war with France August: death of Queen Philippa
1370	Sack of Limoges in the final campaign of the Black Prince
c.1370	Katherine Swynford becomes the mistress of John of Gaunt
1371	September: John of Gaunt marries Constanza (Constance) of Castile, daughter of Pedro
1374	Death of Petrarch
1375	Death of Boccaccio

Year	Life
1377–81	Various journeys to France and Flanders in connection with matters including peace negotiations between England and France and a proposed marriage between King Richard and a French princess
1378	Travels to Lombardy on diplomatic business with Bernabò Visconti, Lord of Milan. Richard II confirms Edward III's annuity of 20 marks; Edward's grant of a pitcher of wine daily is commuted to a second annuity of 20 marks
c.1378–81	Writes *The House of Fame*, *Anelida and Arcite*, *The Parliament of Fowls*, and *Palamon and Arcite* (later adapted as *The Knight's Tale*). Translates the *De Consolatione Philosophiae* of Boethius as the *Boece*
1380	Accused, and acquitted, of the *raptus* (probably either rape or abduction) of Cecily Champain
1381	Birth of a son, Lewis, who was ten when Chaucer wrote the *Treatise of the Astrolabe* for him. Death of Chaucer's mother, Agnes
c.1382–86	Writes *Troilus and Criseyde* and *The Legend of Good Women*
1385–6	Serves as Justice of the Peace for Kent
1386	Elected Knight of the Shire for Kent; retires from Controllership of Customs and relinquishes lease on house in Aldgate
1387	Death of Chaucer's wife, Philippa
c.1387–1400	Writes *The Canterbury Tales*
1388	May: Chaucer's exchequer annuities transferred to John Scalby
1389	Appointed Clerk of the King's Works: responsibilities include construction at Westminster and the Tower of London
1390	Appointed Commissioner of Walls and Ditches, responsible for works on the Thames between Woolwich and Greenwich

Year	Literary and Historical Events
1376	June: death of the Black Prince
1377	June: death of Edward III; accession of Richard II, aged 10
1378	Beginning of the Great Schism: popes in Avignon and Rome. First record of mystery plays in York
late 1370s	Langland revising *Piers Plowman* (the 'B-text')
1381	May: marriage of Richard II to Anne of Bohemia June: the Peasants' Revolt
early 1380s	Langland revising *Piers Plowman* (the 'C-text')
early 1382	Arrival of Queen Anne in England
1382	Official condemnation of the heretical views of John Wycliffe
1385	Death of Joan of Kent, mother of Richard II
1386	Richard II suffers a loss of power
c.1386	John Gower begins his English poem, *Confessio Amantis*, which contains a passage in praise of Chaucer
1388	The Lords Apellant remove some of the King's closest advisers
1389	Richard II regains power

Year	Life
1391	Retires from Clerkship of the King's Works. Appointed Deputy Forester of the Royal Forest of North Petherton, Somerset (a post later held by his son, Thomas). Writes the *Treatise of the Astrolabe*
1393	Awarded £10 by the King for services rendered
1394	Granted an annuity of £20 for life by the King
1395	Chaucer's son Thomas marries the heiress Maud Burghersh
1397	Granted a tun (252 gallons) of wine yearly by the King
1399	Confirmation by Henry IV of Richard's grant, with an additional annuity of 40 marks. Leases a residence in the garden of the Lady Chapel of Westminster Abbey
1400	Death; burial in Westminster Abbey (remains subsequently moved to 'Poets' Corner')

Year	Literary and Historical Events
1394	June: death of Queen Anne
1396	John of Gaunt marries Katherine Swynford
1399	February: death of John of Gaunt September: deposition of Richard II; accession of Henry IV

Introduction

The Canterbury Tales comprises a collection of tales written by Geoffrey Chaucer during the last two decades of the fourteenth century. Though there are other collections of tales from the late Middle Ages, some of which have in common with Chaucer's work the use of a frame story or of more than one narrator, *The Canterbury Tales* has some highly distinctive features – above all the use of a pilgrimage from Southwark to Canterbury as a frame narrative, and the sophisticated development of relationships between tales and among tellers. The work was never finished, and has survived in numerous manuscripts and in a fragmentary state. The surviving fragments are, however, sufficiently substantial and coherent to have provided scholars with ample evidence on which to base a series of deductions about the essential form and nature of the work. Among these, some of the most significant are that *The Canterbury Tales* constitutes a series of tales told by a conspicuously varied group of tellers, linked by passages describing interactions between these tellers; that it is a flexible and expansive work, which deals with a great variety of themes and includes examples of a wide range of genres; and that it is an essentially dynamic work, in which connections and relations between its constituent parts are constantly developing and evolving. The present edition comprises the *General Prologue*, in which Chaucer introduces his tellers and the pilgrimage story, and several comic and bawdy tales, taken from two fragments of *The Canterbury Tales*, the opening fragment (Fragment I) and another from later in the work (Fragment VII).

The *General Prologue* serves to introduce *The Canterbury Tales* and to establish some of its fundamental characteristics. After a formal opening passage, which sets the narrative in spring and suggests, in passing, a paradoxical connection between sexual and spiritual urges, Chaucer introduces a company of individuals, about to set forth on pilgrimage to the shrine of St Thomas Becket in Canterbury Cathedral, who meet at the Tabard Inn, at the southern end of London Bridge in Southwark. Taken together with various aspects of Chaucer's narrative method, the fact that there was an actual

inn of this name in Southwark at the time can encourage the reader
to assume that the *General Prologue* constitutes reportage rather
than fiction. Careful reflection should, however, make it clear that
the account is highly stylized and essentially fictive – though it does
make constant allusion to contemporary objects, issues, and
people. The pilgrims are introduced as a series of individuals,
identified by their professions or trades. While Chaucer asserts that
this procedure is reasonable (line 37), the reasoning that informs it
emerges only in retrospect. Meanwhile, the reader meets roughly
two dozen (fictional) individuals, from a wide range of medieval
society, described in an order which bears some resemblance to a
descending sequence of social rank, without conforming precisely
to it. Other, and various, sequences, groupings, parallels, and
contrasts emerge, among them (in order) the following: a knight,
accompanied by his son (a squire) and personal servant (a
yeoman); three members of the regular orders, a prioress, a monk,
and a friar; a worldly merchant juxtaposed with an unworldly
cleric; several rich and successful professionals, such as a sergeant
at law and a physician; an unconventional businesswoman
contrasted with a dedicated priest, who is linked, in turn, with a
humble ploughman; and, lastly, five rogues – a miller, a manciple, a
reeve, a summoner, and a pardoner – with a common propensity
for cheating the unwary. These descriptions, often termed 'por-
traits' by critics, range in length from nine to over sixty lines, and
vary greatly in content, focus, and emphasis. At the end of this
sequence, the reason for describing the pilgrims becomes apparent:
they will be the tellers in a tale-telling contest to be conducted en
route by the Host, the landlord of the Tabard. In the process, the
pilgrims become tellers, and the terms by which they are known –
'knight', 'squire', etc. – come to be preceded by 'the' rather than 'a'.

Towards the end of the *General Prologue*, Chaucer asserts that he
is bound to report the actual words spoken by these pilgrims,
implicitly claiming reality for them and explicitly disclaiming his
own responsibility for anything they may say (lines 725–42).
Though this assertion is plainly absurd, since Chaucer is the creator
of the pilgrims and thus of everything they say, it may alert the
reader to issues which will prove significant in *The Canterbury Tales*,
especially the authority of the author and the relationship between
the authorial voice and the voices of the various tellers. Chaucer's
disclaimer is followed by the beginning of the tale-telling contest.

The pilgrims are invited by the Host to draw lots in order to determine who will tell the first tale; whether by chance or manipulation (on the part of the Host), the Knight is chosen.

The following tale, told by the Knight, is a romance: long, leisurely in pace, and set in the distant past and in remote and exotic locations, it is as a tale of love and chivalry, in which two aristocratic young men compete for the hand of an aristocratic young woman. In the present edition, 'The Knight's Tale' is omitted, and the text resumes immediately after it finishes. This proves to be an exceptionally significant juncture for *The Canterbury Tales* as a whole: in a passage of less than eighty lines, normally termed *The Miller's Prologue*, some vital evidence about the nature of the work emerges for the first time. Five points, in particular, are of such significance that it will be worth specifying them here. First, the pilgrims respond to *The Knight's Tale*, thus establishing the idea that they constitute a fictional audience within *The Canterbury Tales*. Second, the Miller undermines the Host's attempt to control the order in which the tales shall be told, which suggests that this will not conform to any single principle of ordering but will be subject to a variety of pressures and vicissitudes. Third, the Miller expresses an intention to respond to the tale told by the Knight, summarizing the tale he has in mind, and implying that tales may express the views and values of their tellers, and may provide a means of debate between them. Fourth, in the Reeve's objection to the Miller's summary, and the Miller's response, in which he addresses the Reeve by name, there is a suggestion both of further potential debates and of personal contacts between these pilgrims preceding the narrative. Fifth, the conduct of the Host, the Miller, and the Reeve is broadly in accordance with expectations set up in the preceding *General Prologue*. Thus it becomes apparent that the work will generate dynamic relationships, not just between tellers and their tales, but also between the *General Prologue* and the tales, between the tales, between the tellers, and between the tales and the fictional audience.

At the end of *The Miller's Prologue*, Chaucer reiterates his disclaimer of responsibility, admitting that the Miller and the Reeve will tell the kind of tales one might expect from churls, and asking the reader not to blame the author or to take them too seriously. Though the tales of the Miller and the Reeve are, indeed, bawdy and irreverent, it would, I think, take an unduly sensitive and censorious reader to find anything significantly offensive in them. They both reflect the influence of *fabliau* (plural *fabliaux*). Tales of this genre, mainly but not exclusively from France, are typically short and racy, concerned with sex and trickery, and characterized by comic bawdiness and amoral attitudes. *The Miller's Tale* and *The Reeve's Tale* are indebted to this genre not only for their general tone and manner, but also for such narrative devices as the 'misplaced kiss' in the former and the 'bedswitch' in the latter. Nonetheless, it is important to recognize that Chaucer developed a relatively limited genre to new levels of sophistication in these two tales. The reader's enjoyment is derived, to a significant degree, from the consummate skill and subtlety with which the parallels, contrasts, repetitions, and variations of the narratives are handled. The effect of this is enhanced by the larger fictional context, in which *The Miller's Tale* is intended by its teller as a satiric response to *The Knight's Tale* and interpreted by the Reeve as a personal slight, and *The Reeve's Tale* is intended by its teller as a devastating riposte to the Miller. These interpretations and intentions are typically articulated in the 'links', such as *The Miller's Prologue* (discussed above) and *The Reeve's Prologue* (which connects the tales of the Miller and the Reeve). The Reeve's sense of grievance is finally explained in his prologue, where he states that, since he is a carpenter – a point made initially in the *General Prologue* (line 614) – he suspects that the Miller implies a parallel between him and the cuckolded carpenter John in *The Miller's Tale*. After *The Reeve's Tale*, there is a further link, in which the Cook responds to the preceding tale, and then embarks on his own – which breaks off, however, after only fifty-eight lines. This tale would, it seems, have been another of the *fabliau* type. There is no means of knowing why Chaucer apparently wrote so little of it.

The end of *The Cook's Tale* also brings the end of the first fragment (Fragment I) of *The Canterbury Tales* – which extends to 4420 lines, and comprises, in sequence, the *General Prologue*, *The Knight's Tale*, *The Miller's Prologue and Tale*, *The Reeve's Prologue and Tale*, and *The Cook's Prologue and Tale*. Despite its incompleteness, this substantial fragment of text clearly establishes not just the narrative framework of *The Canterbury Tales*, but also its essentially dynamic, interactive nature, in which tales relate to tellers, tales to tales, and tellers to tellers. These vital principles apply throughout *The Canterbury Tales*, though their relative importance varies.

The other two tales included in the present edition, *The Shipman's Tale* and *The Nun's Priest's Tale*, are found in Fragment VII, and have been selected mainly as further examples of what I have termed 'comic and bawdy tales'. They do, however, also provide some interesting contrasts with the tales from Fragment I. While *The Shipman's Tale* is a tale of the *fabliau* type, and has much in common with the tales of the Miller and the Reeve, *The Nun's Priest's Tale* is an example of another genre, the fable, and, while undeniably comic, could hardly be described as bawdy. Traditionally, the fable will tell an exemplary story, ostensibly from the animal world, in order to illustrate a simple moral lesson about human nature and conduct. Such lessons, though regularly termed 'morals', are often conducive less to being good than to being careful; as such, they have much in common with the lessons often expressed in *fabliaux* (including those by Chaucer). In *The Nun's Priest's Tale*, the simple form of the fable is elaborated with remarkable delicacy and sophistication, so that the judgement of conduct becomes a highly – but comically – problematic issue. This is achieved with a subtle and understated wit, and communicates a striking enjoyment of intellectual play. It is, however, not easy to attribute such characteristics to the teller, since the Nun's Priest is a shadowy figure, implied rather than described in the *General Prologue* (see lines 163–4), who is otherwise mentioned, very briefly, only in the link preceding his tale (not included in the present edition) and the comments of the Host in the epilogue to his tale (which is included). Nor is the relationship between teller and tale straightforward in *The Shipman's Tale*. A careful reading of the opening passage will reveal that it was originally intended for a female teller. Scholars have speculated that Chaucer initially attributed it to the Wife of Bath (described in the *General Prologue* lines 445–76), and that he reassigned it when he wrote the highly distinctive *Wife of Bath's Prologue and Tale*, but failed to complete the revisions necessary for a male teller. Whatever the truth of the matter, the tale as it stands has no particular appropriateness to its teller, though he is described vividly in the *General Prologue* (lines 338–410).

This is a useful corrective to the commonly held notion that an interesting relationship exists between every tale and its teller. What may, however, justly be regarded as a constant characteristic of the work is the richly varied and endlessly engaging interplay between the frame story, the tellers, and the tales. Readers will, I hope, also discover in *The Canterbury Tales* a view of the world characterized by good humour, sharp observation, wisdom without tendentiousness, and true generosity of spirit.

MALCOLM ANDREW

A Note on This Edition

The 'Comic and Bawdy Tales' presented in this edition comprise a small selection from Fragments I and VII of *The Canterbury Tales*. (The fragmentary nature of the work is discussed in the Introduction, above).

Chaucer opens *The Canterbury Tales* with an introduction known as the *General Prologue* – with which this selection also begins. The first tale, that of the Knight, is not included here. The remainder of Fragment I is, however, included complete. This comprises, in order, *The Miller's Prologue and Tale*, *The Reeve's Prologue and Tale* and *The Cook's Prologue and Tale*.

This selection also includes two individual tales from Fragment VII: *The Shipman's Tale* and *The Nun's Preist's Tale and Epilogue*. These are separated in the work as a whole by tales told by three other tellers: The Prioress, the Monk, and Chaucer himself – none of which are included here.

The present edition is based on the original Everyman *Canterbury Tales*, which was edited by A.C. Cawley using a text prepared and revised by F.N. Robinson. The notes and appendices are Cawley's, with revisions and all other material by myself.

MALCOLM ANDREW

Comic and Bawdy Tales

General Prologue

Here bygynneth the Book of the Tales of Caunterbury

WHAN that Aprill with his shoures soote   *sweet*
The droghte of March hath perced to the roote,
And bathed every veyne in swich licour
Of which vertu engendred is the flour;
5 Whan Zephirus eek with his sweete breeth   *also*
Inspired hath in every holt and heeth   *quickened; wood*
The tendre croppes, and the yonge sonne   *shoots*
Hath in the Ram his half cours yronne,
And smale foweles maken melodye,   *birds*
10 That slepen al the nyght with open ye
(So priketh hem nature in hir corages);   *incites; hearts*
Thanne longen folk to goon on pilgrimages,
And palmeres for to seken straunge strondes,
To ferne halwes, kowthe in sondry londes;
15 And specially from every shires ende
Of Engelond to Caunterbury they wende,   *go*
The hooly blisful martir for to seke.   *blessed; visit*
That hem hath holpen whan that they were   *helped*
    seeke.   *sick*
    Bifil that in that seson on a day,
20 In Southwerk at the Tabard as I lay   *stayed*
Redy to wenden on my pilgrymage
To Caunterbury with ful devout corage,

3–4 And bathed every sap-vessel in moisture, by virtue of which the flower is produced.
7–8 The young sun (i.e. the sun at the beginning of its annual journey) has completed the second half of its course in the Ram. (In other words the sun had left the zodiacal sign Aries, which it did in Chaucer's time on 11th April.)
13 And palmers to visit foreign shores.
14 To distant shrines, well known in different lands.
17 i.e. St Thomas Becket.
20 This is an allusion to an actual inn, the Tabard, situated in Southwark, just south of London bridge. A *tabard* was a short, sleeveless embroidered coat worn by heralds.

At nyght was come into that hostelrye
Wel nyne and twenty in a compaignye,   *at least*
25 Of sondry folk, by aventure yfalle
In felaweshipe, and pilgrimes were they alle,
That toward Caunterbury wolden ryde.   *intended to*
The chambres and the stables weren wyde,
And wel we weren esed atte beste.
30 And shortly, whan the sonne was to reste,   *(gone) to rest*
So hadde I spoken with hem everichon   *each one*
That I was of hir felaweshipe anon,
And made forward erly for to ryse,   *agreement*
To take oure wey ther as I yow devyse.
35   But nathelees, whil I have tyme and   *nevertheless*
space,   *opportunity*
Er that I ferther in this tale pace,   *before; proceed*
Me thynketh it acordaunt to resoun
To telle yow al the condicioun
Of ech of hem, so as it semed me,
40 And whiche they weren, and of what degree,
And eek in what array that they were inne;   *attire*
And at a knyght than wol I first bigynne.
A KNYGHT ther was, and that a worthy man,
That fro the tyme that he first bigan
45 To riden out, he loved chivalrie,   *to go campaigning*
Trouthe and honour, fredom and curteisie.
Ful worthy was he in his lordes werre,   *war*
And therto hadde he riden, no man ferre,   *also; farther*
As wel in cristendom as in hethenesse,   *heathendom*
50 And evere honoured for his worthynesse.
At Alisaundre he was whan it was wonne.
Ful ofte tyme he hadde the bord bigonne
Aboven alle nacions in Pruce;   *Prussia*
In Lettow hadde he reysed and in Ruce,
55 No Cristen man so ofte of his degree.
In Gernade at the seege eek hadde he be
Of Algezir, and riden in Belmarye.

25 By chance met together.
29 And we were excellently entertained.
34 To where I tell you of.
37 It seems to me to be in order.
40 And what sort of men they were.
46 *Trouthe*, fidelity, loyalty; *fredom*, liberality; *curteisie*, gracious and considerate conduct.
51 The Saracen stronghold of Alexandria was taken by Pierre de Lusignan, King of Cyprus, in 1365.
52 He had very often sat in the seat of honour at table.
54 He had campaigned with the Teutonic knights against the barbarians of Lithuania and Russia.
56–7 He had taken part in the siege and capture of the Moorish citadel of Algezir in Granada (1344); *Belmarye*, Benmarin, a Moorish kingdom in North Africa.

At Lyeys was he and at Satalye,
Whan they were wonne: and in the Grete See   *Mediterranean*
60 At many a noble armee hadde he be.   *armed expedition*
At mortal batailles hadde he been fiftene,
And foughten for oure feith at Tramyssene
In lystes thries, and ay slayn his foo.   *lists; thrice*
This ilke worthy knyght hadde been also   *same*
65 Somtyme with the lord of Palatye   *once; Palatia*
Agayn another hethen in Turkye,
And everemoore he hadde a sovereyn prys;
And though that he were worthy, he was wys,   *eminent; wise*
And of his port as meeke as is a mayde.   *bearing*
70 He nevere yet no vileynye ne sayde
In all his lyf unto no maner wight.
He was a verray, parfit gentil knyght.
But, for to tellen yow of his array,   *outfit*
His hors were goode, but he was nat gay.   *horses*
75 Of fustian he wered a gypon
Al bismotered with his habergeon,
For he was late ycome from his viage,   *military expedition*
And wente for to doon his pilgrymage.
With hym ther was his sone, a yong SQUIER,   *squire*
80 A lovyere and a lusty bacheler,
With lokkes crulle as they were leyd in presse.
Of twenty yeer of age he was, I gesse.
Of his stature he was of evene lengthe,   *medium height*
And wonderly delyvere, and of greet   *wonderfully active*
    strengthe.
85 And he hadde been somtyme in chyvachie   *on cavalry raids*
In Flaundres, in Artoys, and Pycardie,
And born hym weel, as of so litel space,
In hope to stonden in his lady grace.
Embrouded was he, as it were a meede   *meadow*
90 Al ful of fresshe floures, whyte and reede.
Synginge he was, or floytynge, al the day;   *fluting*
He was as fressh as is the month of May.
Short was his gowne, with sleves longe and wyde.
Wel koude he sitte on hors and faire ryde.   *excellently*

58 *Lyeys, Satalye*, Ayas (in Armenia) and Attalia (in Asia Minor), captured by
    de Lusignan in 1367 and 1361 respectively.
62 *Tramyssene*, Tlemcen in Algeria.
67 And always he had an outstanding reputation.
70–2 He had never in all his life spoken rudely to any sort of person. He was a
    true, complete, and noble knight.
75–6 He wore a surcoat of fustian (a course material of cotton and flax) all
    spotted with rust from his coat of mail.
80 A lover and a lusty young knight.
81 As curly as if they had been pressed by a curling-iron.
87 And conducted himself well, considering the short time of his service.

95 He koude songes make and wel endite,	
Juste and eek daunce, and weel purtreye	*joust; draw*
and write.	
So hoote he lovede that by nyghtertale	*hotly; night*
He sleep namoore than dooth a nyghtyngale.	
Curteis he was, lowely, and servysable,	
100 And carf biforn his fader at the table.	
A YEMAN hadde he and servantz namo	
At that tyme, for hym liste ride so,	*he chose to*
And he was clad in cote and hood of grene.	
A sheef of pecok arwes, bright and kene,	
105 Under his belt he bar ful thriftily,	*carefully*
(Wel koude he dresse his takel yemanly:	
His arwes drouped noght with fetheres lowe)	
And in his hand he baar a myghty bowe.	
A not heed hadde he, with a broun visage.	*close-cropped*
110 Of wodecraft wel koude he al the usage.	*knew*
Upon his arm he baar a gay bracer,	
And by his syde a swerd and a bokeler,	
And on that oother syde a gay daggere	
Harneised wel and sharp as point of spere;	*mounted*
115 A Cristopher on his brest of silver sheene.	
An horn he bar, the bawdryk was of grene;	*baldric*
A forster was he, soothly, as I gesse.	*forester; truly*
Ther was also a Nonne, a PRIORESSE,	
That of hir smylyng was ful symple and	*unaffected*
coy;	*modest*
120 Hire gretteste ooth was but by Seinte Loy;	*Eligius*
And she was cleped madame Eglentyne.	*called*
Ful weel she soong the service dyvyne,	
Entuned in hir nose ful semely,	
And Frenssh she spak ful faire and fetisly,	*elegantly*
125 After the scole of Stratford atte Bowe,	
For Frenssh of Parys was to hire unknowe.	*unknown*
At mete wel ytaught was she with alle:	*table; moreover*
She leet no morsel from hir lippes falle,	

95 He was good at composing the music and words of songs.
99 He was courteous, humble, and willing to be of service.
101 *Yeman*, attendant; *he*, i.e. the Knight; *namo*, no other.
104 *pecok arwes*, arrows with peacock feathers.
106–7 He well knew how to prepare his tackle in yeoman-like fashion: there were no flattened feathers to make his arrows droop in flight.
111 *bracer*, guard for the bow-arm.
115 *Cristopher*, figure of St Christopher, the patron saint of foresters; *sheene*, bright.
123 Intoned in her nose in a very seemly manner.
125 The Prioress spoke French with the accent she had learned in her convent (the Benedictine nunnery of St Leonard's near Stratford-Bow in Middlesex).

Ne wette hir fyngres in hir sauce depe;	nor; deeply

130 Wel koude she carie a morsel and wel kepe   *take good care*
That no drope ne fille upon hire brest.
In curteisie was set ful muchel hir lest.
Hir over-lippe wyped she so clene
That in hir coppe ther was no ferthyng sene   *cup; spot*
135 Of grece, whan she dronken hadde hir draughte.
Ful semely after hir mete she raughte.   *food; reached*
And silterly she was of greet desport,
And ful plesaunt, and amyable of port,
And peyned hire to countrefete cheere
140 Of court, and to been estatlich of manere,
And to ben holden digne of reverence.   *held worthy*
But, for to speken of hire conscience,   *tender feeling*
She was so charitable and so pitous   *compassionate*
She wolde wepe, if that she saugh a mous
145 Kaught in a trappe, if it were deed or bledde.   *if it bled*
Of smale houndes hadde she that she fedde
With rosted flessh, or milk and wastel-breed.
But soore wepte she if oon of hem were deed,
Or if men smoot it with a yerde smerte;
150 And al was conscience and tendre herte.
Ful semyly hir wympul pynched was,   *wimple; pleated*
Hir nose tretys, hir eyen greye as glas,   *well shaped; eyes*
Hir mouth ful smal, and therto softe and reed;
But sikerly she hadde a fair forheed;
155 It was almoost a spanne brood, I trowe;   *think*
For, hardily, she was nat undergrowe.
Ful fetys was hir cloke, as I was war.
Of smal coral aboute hire arm she bar   *carried*
A peire of bedes, gauded al with grene,
60 And theron heng a brooch of gold ful sheene,
On which ther was first write a crowned A,
And after *Amor vincit omnia.*
     Another NONNE with hire hadde she,
That was hir chapeleyne, and preestes thre.
165   A MONK ther was, a fair for the maistrie,

132 She took great pleasure in polite manners.
137 And certainly she was a very cheerful person.
139–40 She took pains to imitate courtly behaviour, and to be dignified in her
    bearing.
147 *wastel-breed*, fine wheat bread.
149 Or if anyone struck it sharply with a stick.
156 For, certainly, she was not small in stature.
157 I noticed that her cloak was very elegant.
159 A rosary with 'gauds' (i.e. large beads for the Paternosters) of green.
161 *crowned A*, capital A with a crown above it.
164 One of the three priests later tells *The Nun's Priest's Tale.*
165 A most excellent one.

An outridere, that lovede venerie,
A manly man, to been an abbot able.   *fit*
Ful many a deyntee hors hadde he in stable,   *valuable*
And whan he rood, men myghte his brydel heere
170 Gynglen in a whistlynge wynd als cleere
And eek as loude as dooth the chapel belle.
Ther as this lord was kepere of the celle,
The reule of seint Maure or of seint Beneit,
By cause that it was old and somdel streit   *somewhat strict*
175 This ilke Monk leet olde thynges pace,   *slide*
And heeld after the newe world the space.
He yaf nat of that text a pulled hen,
That seith that hunters ben nat hooly men,
Ne that a monk, whan he is recchelees,
180 Is likned til a fissh that is waterlees,—   *to*
This is to seyn, a monk out of his cloystre.
But thilke text heeld he nat worth an oystre;   *that*
And I seyde his opinion was good.
What sholde he studie and make hymselven   *why*
       wood,   *mad*
185 Upon a book in cloystre alwey to poure,
Or swynken with his handes, and laboure,   *toil*
As Austyn bit? How shal the world be served?
Lat Austyn have his swynk to hym reserved!   *himself*
Therfore he was a prikasour aright:
190 Grehoundes he hadde as swift as fowel in flight;
Of prikyng and of huntyng for the hare
Was al his lust, for no cost wolde he spare.   *pleasure*
I seigh his sleves purfiled at the hond
With grys, and that the fyneste of a lond;
195 And, for to festne his hood under his chyn,
He hadde of gold ywroght a ful curious pyn;
A love-knotte in the gretter ende ther was.
His heed was balled, that shoon as any glas,

166 *outridere*, monk who rode out to supervise the estates of a monastery;
     venerie, hunting.
172 *Ther as*, where; *celle*, subordinate monastery.
173 St Maurus was a disciple of St Benedict, who founded the Benedictine order
     in 529 and drew up the rule of life to be observed by it.
176 And followed the new order of things meanwhile.
177 He did not value that text at the price of a plucked hen.
179 *recchelees*, careless, i.e. neglectful of monastic discipline.
187 *Austyn*, St Augustine of Hippo (345–430); *How shal the world be served?*, i.e.
     who else is fitted to do all the valuable secular work now done by the clergy?
189 He was a real hard galloper.
191 *prikyng*, tracking of a hare by its footprints.
193–4 Trimmed at the cuff with costly grey fur.
196 He had a most elaborate brooch made of gold.
197 There was a true-love knot at the larger end.

And eek his face, as he hadde been enoynt. *anointed*
200 He was a lord ful fat and in good poynt; *condition*
His eyen stepe, and rollynge in his heed, *prominent*
That stemed as a forneys of a leed;
His bootes souple, his hors in greet estaat. *form*
Now certeinly he was a fair prelaat; *fine*
205 He was nat pale as a forpyned goost. *tormented*
A fat swan loved he best of any roost.
His palfrey was as broun as is a berye.
 A FRERE ther was, a wantowne and a merye, *jovial*
A lymytour, a ful solempne man.
210 In alle the ordres foure is noon that kan *knows*
So muchel of daliaunce and fair langage. *gossip; flattery*
He hadde maad ful many a mariage
Of yonge wommen at his owene cost.
Unto his ordre he was a noble post. *pillar*
215 Ful wel biloved and famulier was he
With frankeleyns over al in his contree,
And eek with worthy wommen of the toun;
For he hadde power of confessioun,
As seyde hymself, moore than a curat, *parish priest*
220 For of his ordre he was licenciat.
Ful swetely herde he confessioun,
And plesaunt was his absolucioun:
He was an esy man to yeve penaunce,
Ther as he wiste to have a good pitaunce.
225 For unto a povre ordre for to yive *poor*
Is signe that a man is wel yshryve; *shriven*
For if he yaf, he dorste make avaunt,
He wiste that a man was repentaunt; *knew*
For many a man so hard is of his herte,
230 He may nat wepe, althogh hym soore smerte.
Therfore in stede of wepynge and preyeres
Men moote yeve silver to the povre freres. *must give*

202 That (i.e. his eyes) glowed like the furnace under a cauldron.
209 A limiter (i.e. friar licensed to beg within a certain district), a very imposing man.
210 The four orders of friars were the Dominicans (Black Friars), Franciscans (Grey Friars), Carmelites (White Friars), and Augustinians (Austin Friars).
212–13 These lines mean that the Friar found husbands or dowries for the many young women he had seduced.
216 With franklins everywhere in his district.
217 With women of standing in the towns.
218–20 i.e. he had a licence from his order to hear confessions and to grant absolution for serious offences which the parish priest had to refer to his bishop.
224 Where he knew he would receive generous alms.
227 For if a man gave freely, he (the Friar) dared to assert.
230 He cannot weep, although his sin hurts him grievously.

His typet was ay farsed ful of knyves   *tippet; stuffed*
And pynnes, for to yeven faire wyves.
235 And certeinly he hadde a murye note: *pleasant voice*
Wel koude he synge and pleyen on a rote;
Of yeddynges he baar outrely the pris.
. His nekke whit was as the flour-de-lys;
Therto he strong was as a champioun.   *professional fighter*
240 He knew the tavernes wel in every toun
And everich hostiler and tappestere
Bet than a lazar or a beggestere;
For unto swich a worthy man as he
Acorded nat, as by his facultee,
245 To have with sike lazars aqueyntaunce.
It is nat honest, it may nat avaunce,
For to deelen with no swich poraille,
But al with riche and selleres of vitaille.
And over al, ther as profit sholde arise,
250 Curteis he was and lowely of servyse.   *courteous; humble*
Ther nas no man nowher so vertuous.
He was the beste beggere in his hous;
For thogh a wydwe hadde noght a sho,
So plesaunt was his 'In principio,'
255 Yet wolde he have a ferthyng, er he wente.   *small gift*
His purchas was wel bettre than his rente.
And rage he koude, as it were right a whelp.
In love-dayes ther koude he muchel help,
For ther he was nat lyk a cloysterer   *resident of a cloister*
260 With a thredbare cope, as is a povre scoler,   *out-door cloak*
But he was lyk a maister or a pope.   *master of arts*
Of double worstede was his semycope,   *short cloak*
That rounded as a belle out of the presse.
Somwhat he lipsed, for his wantownesse,

236 *rote*, stringed instrument.
237 In singing popular songs he excelled all others.
241–2 And every innkeeper and barmaid better than a leper or a beggar-
woman.
244 It was not fitting, in view of his profession.
246–8 It is not respectable or profitable to have dealings with such poor people,
but only with rich people and licensed victuallers.
249 And wherever profit was likely to arise.
251 Nowhere was there any man so capable.
254 *In principio*, the opening words of St John's Gospel, which were regarded in
the Middle Ages as a charm against evil.
256 The proceeds of his begging were much better than his income. (That is to
say, although he was a friar and so had no regular income, he managed to
pick up quite a lot.)
257 He could play wantonly, just like a puppy.
258 He could give much help by acting as umpire on love-days (i.e. days
appointed for settling disputes by arbitration).
263 That was a rounded as a bell out of the mould.
264 He lisped a little, by way of affectation.

265 To make his Englissh sweete upon his tonge;
     And in his harpyng, whan that he hadde songe,
     His eyen twynkled in his heed aryght   *just*
     As doon the sterres in the frosty nyght.
     This worthy lymytour was cleped Huberd.   *called Hubert*
270   A MARCHANT was ther with a forked berd,
     In mottelee, and hye on horse he sat;   *motley*
     Upon his heed a Flaundryssh bever hat,
     His bootes clasped faire and fetisly   *elegantly*
     His resons he spak ful solempnely,   *opinions*
275 Sownynge alwey th'encrees of his   *proclaiming*
         wynnyng.   *profits*
     He wolde the see were kept for any thyng
     Bitwixe Middelburgh and Orewelle.
     Wel koude he in eschaunge sheeldes selle.
     This worthy man ful wel his wit bisette:
280 Ther wiste no wight that he was in dette,   *knew; person*
     So estatly was he of his governaunce
     With his bargaynes and with his chevyssaunce.
     For sothe he was a worthy man with alle,
     But, sooth to seyn, I noot how men hym calle.
285   A CLERK ther was of Oxenford also,   *student*
     That unto logyk hadde longe ygo.
     As leene was his hors as is a rake,
     And he nas nat right fat, I undertake,
     But looked holwe, and therto sobrely.   *serious*
290 Ful thredbare was his overeste courtepy;   *short outer coat*
     For he hadde geten hym yet no benefice,
     Ne was so worldly for to have office.   *secular employment*
     For hym was levere have at his beddes heed   *he would rather*
     Twenty bookes, clad in blak or reed,   *bound*
295 Of Aristotle and his philosophie,
     Than robes riche, or fithele, or gay sautrie.   *fiddle; psaltery*
     But al be that he was a philosophre,
     Yet hadde he but litel gold in cofre;

272 Upon his head a Flemish hat of beaver fur.
276–7 He wished the sea to be guarded at all costs between Middelburg (in
     Holland) and Orwell (near Harwich in Suffolk).
278 He well knew how to sell French crowns at a profit.
279 Used his wits to the best advantage.
281–2 He conducted himself with such dignity in making his bargains and
     loans.
284 But, to tell the truth, I don't know what he is called.
286 Who had long since proceeded to the study of logic. (The Clerk was a
     university student who had taken the bachelor's degree and was now studying
     for the master's degree.)
297 But although he was a philosopher. (There is a pun here on the word
     'philosopher', which could also be used of an alchemist, who spent his time
     trying to transmute baser metals into gold.)

But al that he myghte of his freendes hente,	*get*
300 On bookes and on lernynge he it spente,	
And bisily gan for the soules preye	*did*
Of hem that yaf hym wherwith to scoleye.	*gave; study*
Of studie took he moost cure and moost heede.	*care*
Noght o word spak he moore than was neede,	
305 And that was seyd in forme and reverence,	
And short and quyk and ful of hy sentence;	
Sownynge in moral vertu was his speche,	
And gladly wolde he lerne and gladly teche.	
A SERGEANT OF THE LAWE, war and wys,	
310 That often hadde been at the Parvys,	
Ther was also, ful riche of excellence.	
Discreet he was and of greet reverence –	*dignity*
He semed swich, his wordes weren so wise.	
Justice he was ful often in assise,	
315 By patente and by pleyn commissioun.	
For his science and for his heigh renoun,	*knowledge*
Of fees and robes hadde he many oon.	*a one*
So greet a purchasour was nowher noon:	*buyer of land*
Al was fee symple to hym in effect;	
320 His purchasyng myghte nat been infect.	
Nowher so bisy a man as he ther nas,	
And yet he semed bisier than he was.	
In termes hadde he caas and doomes alle	
That from the tyme of kyng William were falle.	
325 Therto he koude endite, and make a thyng,	
Ther koude no wight pynche at his writyng;	*find fault with*
And every statut koude he pleyn by rote.	
He rood but hoomly in a medlee cote	*motley*
Girt with a ceint of silk, with barres smale;	
330 Of his array telle I no lenger tale.	

305 Formally and respectfully.
306 Lively and full of deep meaning.
307 i.e. his conversation was of an edifying nature.
309 The Sergeants-at-Law were high legal officers, from whom the judges of the
   King's courts were chosen; *war and wys*, cautious and prudent.
310 *Parvys*, the porch of St Paul's, where lawyers met their clients for
   consultation. (Another possible meaning is that he had often presided at the
   academic disputations of students in the inns of court.)
314–15 He had very often been a judge at the assizes, appointed by the King's
   letters patent and by a warrant giving him jurisdiction in all kinds of cases.
319–20 i.e. he always got absolute possession of any land he bought; his title to
   it could never be proved defective.
321 Nowhere was there so busy a man as he was.
323–4 He had an accurate knowledge of all the legal cases and judgments
   which had come about since the time of William the Conqueror.
325 Moreover he knew how to write and draw up a legal document.
327 He knew completely by heart.
329 A girdle of silk with narrow ornamental bars.

A FRANKELEYN was in his compaignye.
Whit was his berd as is the dayesye;
Of his complexioun he was sangwyn.   *temperament*
Wel loved he by the morwe a sop in wyn;
335   To lyven in delit was evere his wone,   *wont*
For he was Epicurus owene sone,   *son*
That heeld opinioun that pleyn delit   *pure delight*
Was verray felicitee parfit.
An housholdere, and that a greet, was he;
340   Seint Julian he was in his contree.
His breed, his ale, was alweys after oon;
A bettre envyned man was nowher noon.
Withoute bake mete was nevere his hous
Of fissh and flessh, and that so plentevous,
345   It snewed in his hous of mete and drynke,   *food*
Of alle deyntees that men koude thynke.   *delicacies*
After the sondry sesons of the yeer,
So chaunged he his mete and his soper.   *dinner*
Ful many a fat partrich hadde he in muwe,   *coop*
350   And many a breem and many a luce in stuwe.   *pike; fishpond*
Wo was his cook but if his sauce were
Poynaunt and sharp, and redy al his geere.
His table dormant in his halle alway
Stood redy covered al the longe day.
355   At sessiouns ther was he lord and sire;
Ful ofte tyme he was knyght of the shire.
An anlaas and a gipser al of silk   *dagger; pouch*
Heeng at his girdel, whit as morne milk.   *morning*
A shirreve hadde he been, and a countour.
360   Was nowher swich a worthy vavasour.   *landowner*
    AN HABERDASSHERE and a CARPENTER,
A WEBBE, a DYERE, and a TAPYCER, —
And they were clothed alle in o lyveree
Of a solempne and a greet fraternitee.

331   A franklin was a substantial landowner of the gentry class.
334   Early in the morning a piece of bread dipped in wine.
336   i.e. a follower of the Greek philosopher Epicurus (c. 341–270 B.C.).
340   *Seint Julian*, the patron saint of hospitality; *contree*, district.
341   Always of one standard, i.e. uniformly good.
342   No one anywhere had a wine cellar better stocked than his.
351–2   Woe to his cook if his sauce were not piquant and his utensils all ready.
353   *table dormant*, fixed table (as distinct from one on trestles).
355   He presided at sessions of justices of the peace.
356   *knyght of the shire*, representative of the county in parliament.
359   *shirreve*, sheriff, a high administrative officer representing the royal
      authority in a shire; *countour*, auditor.
362   *Webbe*, weaver; *Tapycer*, tapestry-maker.
363–4   Since they belonged to different trades, the one livery they all wore must
      have been that of a religious guild or fraternity.

365 Ful fressh and newe hir geere apiked was;	*adorned*
Hir knyves were chaped noght with bras	*mounted*
But al with silver; wroght ful clene and weel	*neatly*
Hire girdles and hir pouches everydeel.	*in every detail*
Wel semed ech of hem a fair burgeys	
370 To sitten in a yeldehalle on a deys.	*guildhall; dais*
Everich, for the wisdom that he kan,	
Was shaply for to been an alderman.	*fit*
For catel hadde they ynogh and rente,	*property; revenue*
And eek hir wyves wolde it wel assente;	
375 And elles certeyn were they to blame.	
It is ful fair to been ycleped 'madame,'	*called*
And goon to vigilies al bifore,	
And have a mantel roialliche ybore.	*borne*
A COOK they hadde with hem for the nones	*on purpose*
380 To boille the chiknes with the marybones,	
And poudre-marchant tart and galyngale.	
Wel koude he knowe a draughte of Londoun ale.	
He koude rooste, and sethe, and broille, and frye,	
Maken mortreux, and wel bake a pye.	*thick soups*
385 But greet harm was it, as it thoughte me,	*pity; seemed to me*
That on his shyne a mormal hadde he.	*sore*
For blankmanger, that made he with the beste.	
A SHIPMAN was ther, wonynge fer by weste;	
For aught I woot, he was of Dertemouthe.	*know*
390 He rood upon a rouncy, as he kouthe,	
In a gowne of faldyng to the knee.	*coarse woollen cloth*
A daggere hangynge on a laas hadde he	*cord*
Aboute his nekke, under his arm adoun.	
The hoote somer hadde maad his hewe al broun;	
395 And certeinly he was a good felawe.	
Ful many a draughte of wyn had he ydrawe	
Fro Burdeux-ward, whil that the chapman sleep.	
Of nyce conscience took he no keep.	

371 Each one, for his wisdom (lit. for the wisdom that he knows).
377 *vigilies*, vigils, i.e. services held on the eve of a religious festival; *al bifore*, before everyone else.
381 *poudre-marchant tart*, tart flavouring powder; *galyngale*, spice prepared from the root of sweet cyperus.
382 He well knew how to recognize.
387 *blankmanger*, 'white food' made from minced fowl, cream, rice, almonds, etc.
388 Living far to the west.
390 He rode on a cob, as well as he knew how.
395 *good felawe*. This phrase often carries a suggestion of rascality, as here and in line 650 below.
396–7 Had he stolen on the voyage home from Bordeaux, while the merchant was sleeping.
398 He had no time for tender feelings.

If that he faught, and hadde the hyer hond, *upper*
400 By water he sente hem hoom to every lond.
But of his craft to rekene wel his tydes, *skill*
His stremes, and his daungers hym bisides, *round about him*
His herberwe, and his moone, his lodemenage,
Ther nas noon swich from Hulle to Cartage. *Cartegena*
405 Hardy he was and wys to undertake;
With many a tempest hadde his berd been shake.
He knew alle the havenes, as they were,
Fro Gootlond to the cape of Fynystere,
And every cryke in Britaigne and in Spayne. *Brittany*
410 His barge ycleped was the Maudelayne. *ship; Magdalen*
 With us ther was a DOCTOUR OF PHISIK;
In al this world ne was ther noon hym lik,
To speke of phisik and of surgerye,
For he was grounded in astronomye. *astrology*
415 He kepte his pacient a ful greet deel
In houres by his magyk natureel.
Wel koude he fortunen the ascendent
Of his ymages for his pacient.
He knew the cause of everich maladye,
420 Were it of hoot, or coold, or moyste, or drye,
And where they engendred, and of what humour.
He was a verray, parfit praktisour:
The cause yknowe, and of his harm the roote, *known; its*
Anon he yaf the sike man his boote. *remedy*
425 Ful redy hadde he his apothecaries
To sende hym drogges and his letuaries, *medicaments*
For ech of hem made oother for to wynne—
Hir frendshipe nas nat newe to bigynne.

400 i.e. he drowned his prisoners.
403 His harbours, phases of the moon, and pilotage.
405 He was bold and yet prudent in what he undertook.
408 *Gootlond*, Gotland, an island off the coast of Sweden; *Fynystere*, Finisterre, a cape in north-west Spain.
415–18 He watched his patient very carefully and chose by natural magic (as distinct from black magic) the right astrological hours for giving him treatment. He knew exactly how to find a favourable ascendant for making images in the interests of his patient. (The 'images' may have been either effigies of the patient or astrological emblems, made in this instance to benefit the sick person.)
420 These, according to medieval physiology, are the four chief elements of the body, which combine to produce the four humours or bodily moistures. It was believed that diseases are caused by an excess of one or more of the humours: *blood* in the sanguine, *phlegm* in the phlegmatic, *choler* or yellow-red bile in choleric persons, *melancholy* or black bile in the melancholic.
422 He was a true, complete practitioner.
427 Each put money into the other's pocket – the doctor by prescribing cheap drugs, the apothecary by overcharging for them.

    Wel knew he the olde Esculapius,
430 And Deyscorides, and eek Rufus,
    Olde Ypocras, Haly, and Galyen,   *Hippocrates; Galen*
    Serapion, Razis, and Avycen,   *Avicenna*
    Averrois, Damascien, and Constantyn,
    Bernard, and Gatesden, and Gilbertyn.
435 Of his diete mesurable was he,   *temperate*
    For it was of no superfluitee,
    But of greet norissyng and digestible.
    His studie was but litel on the Bible.
    In sangwyn and in pers he clad was al,
440 Lyned with taffata and with sendal;   *fine silk*
    And yet he was but esy of dispence;   *thrifty*
    He kepte that he wan in pestilence.   *the plague*
    For gold in phisik is a cordial,
    Therefore he lovede gold in special.
445   A good WIF was ther of biside BATHE, *from near Bath*
    But she was somdel deef, and that was scathe. *a pity*
    Of clooth-makyng she hadde swich an haunt, *skill*
    She passed hem of Ypres and of Gaunt. *surpassed; Ghent*
    In al the parisshe wif ne was ther noon
450 That to the offrynge bifore hire sholde goon;
    And if ther dide, certeyn so wrooth was she, *certainly*
    That she was out of alle charitee.
    Hir coverchiefs ful fyne weren of ground;
    I dorste swere they weyeden ten pound
455 That on a Sonday weren upon hir heed.
    Hir hosen weren of fyn scarlet reed,   *stockings*
    Ful streite yteyd, and shoes ful moyste and newe.
    Boold was hir face, and fair, and reed of hewe.
    She was a worthy womman al hir lyve:
460 Housbondes at chirche dore she hadde fyve,
    Withouten oother compaignye in youthe,—   *besides*
    But therof nedeth nat to speke as nowthe.   *at present*
    And thries hadde she been at Jerusalem;

429–34 These medical authorities range from the mythical father of medicine, Aesculapius, to English and French physicians of the 13th and 14th centuries (Gilbertus Anglicus, Bernard of Gordon, and John of Gaddesden). They include great medical authorities from ancient Greece and Rome and from the Arab world of the 9th to the 12th centuries.

443 Gold was held to be a sovereign remedy by medieval physicians. This, Chaucer ironically observes, is why the doctor loved gold so much.

449–50 No woman had to go to the offering before her. (The congregation went up in order of rank to make their offerings to the priest.)

453 Her head-dresses were of a very fine texture.

457 *streite yteyd*, tightly fastened; *moyste*, supple.

460 A medieval marriage was legalized in the church porch and followed by a nuptial mass at the altar.

	She hadde passed many a straunge strem;	*foreign river*
465	At Rome she hadde been, and at Boloigne,	
	In Galice at Seint-Jame, and at Coloigne.	
	She koude muchel of wandrynge by the weye.	*knew a lot*
	Gat-tothed was she, soothly for to seye.	*gap-toothed*
	Upon an amblere esily she sat,	*ambling horse*
470	Ywympled wel, and on hir heed an hat	
	As brood as is a bokeler or a targe;	*buckler; shield*
	A foot-mantel aboute hir hipes large,	*outer skirt*
	And on hir feet a paire of spores sharpe.	
	In felaweshipe wel koude she laughe and carpe.	*talk*
475	Of remedies of love she knew per chaunce,	
	For she koude of that art the olde daunce.	
	A good man was ther of religioun,	
	And was a povre PERSOUN OF A TOUN,	*village priest*
	But riche he was of hooly thoght and werk.	
480	He was also a lerned man, a clerk,	
	That Cristes gospel trewely wolde preche;	
	His parisshens devoutly wolde he teche.	*parishioners*
	Benygne he was, and wonder diligent,	*wonderfully*
	And in adversitee ful pacient,	
485	And swich he was ypreved ofte sithes.	*oftentimes*
	Ful looth were hym to cursen for his tithes,	
	But rather wolde he yeven, out of doute,	*without doubt*
	Unto his povre parisshens aboute	
	Of his offryng and eek of his substaunce.	
490	He koude in litel thyng have suffisaunce.	*sufficiency*
	Wyd was his parisshe, and houses fer asonder,	
	But he ne lefte nat, for reyn ne thonder,	
	In siknesse nor in meschief to visite	*adversity*
	The ferreste in his parisshe, muche	*farthest; great and small*
	and lite,	
495	Upon his feet, and in his hand a staf.	
	This noble ensample to his sheep he yaf,	
	That first he wroghte, and afterward he taughte.	
	Out of the gospel he tho wordes caughte,	
	And this figure he added eek therto,	*figure of speech*
500	That if gold ruste, what shal iren do?	

465–6 She had visited the image of the Virgin at Boulogne, the shrine of St
James at Compostella (in Galicia, Spain), and the shrine of the Magi at
Cologne.
470 Covered with a wimple.
475 She knew the cures for love without a doubt. (The allusion is to Ovid's
Remedia Amoris.)
476 i.e. she knew all the tricks of the trade.
486 He was most unwilling to have anyone excommunicated for not paying his
tithes.
497 He first practised good works himself, and then taught others to do the
same.
498 He took those words out of the Gospel (Matt. v. 19).

For if a preest be foul, on whom we truste,   *vicious*
No wonder is a lewed man to ruste;   *ignorant*
And shame it is, if a prest take keep,
A shiten shepherde and a clene sheep.   *dirty*
505 Wel oghte a preest ensample for to yive,
By his clennesse, how that his sheep sholde lyve.
He sette nat his benefice to hyre
And leet his sheep encombred in the myre   *nor left*
And ran to Londoun unto Seinte Poules   *nor ran*
510 To seken hym a chaunterie for soules,
Or with a bretherhed to been witholde;
But dwelt at hoom, and kepte wel his   *took good care of*
    folde,
So that the wolf ne made it nat myscarie;
He was a shepherde and noght a mercenarie.   *hireling*
515 And though he hooly were and vertuous,
He was to synful men nat despitous,   *scornful*
Ne of his speche daungerous ne digne,   *arrogant; disdainful*
But in his techyng discreet and benygne.   *courteous; kind*
To drawen folk to hevene by fairnesse,   *goodness of life*
520 By good ensample, this was his bisynesse.
But it were any persone obstinat,   *if there was*
What so he were, of heigh or lough estat,   *whatever*
Hym wolde he snybben sharply for the nonys.
A bettre preest I trowe that nowher noon ys.
525 He waited after no pompe and reverence,   *looked for*
Ne maked him a spiced conscience,
But Cristes loore and his apostles twelve
He taughte, but first he folwed it hymselve.
    With hym ther was a PLOWMAN, was his   *(who) was*
        brother,
530 That hadde ylad of dong ful many a fother;   *carted; load*
A trewe swynkere and a good was he,   *labourer*
Lyvynge in pees and parfit charitee.
God loved he best with al his hoole herte
At alle tymes, thogh him gamed or smerte,
535 And thanne his neighebor right as hymselve.
He wolde thresshe, and therto dyke and delve,   *ditch; dig*
For Cristes sake, for every povre wight,
Withouten hire, if it lay in his myght.   *wages*

503 If a priest will but take heed.
507 He did not hire out his benefice.
510 To try to get a chantry, i.e. an endowment for a priest to sing masses for the
     soul of a dead person.
511 Or to be retained as chaplain by a guild.
523 He would rebuke him very sharply.
526 Nor was he too fastidious (in his dealings with his flock).
527 But the doctrine of Christ and his twelve apostles.
529 *brother*, i.e. fellow Christian.
534 Whether it gave him pleasure or pain.

His tithes payde he ful faire and wel,
540 Bothe of his propre swynk and his catel.
In a tabard he rood upon a mere.   *labourer's smock; mare*
    Ther was also a REVE, and a MILLERE,
A SOMNOUR, and a PARDONER also,
A MAUNCIPLE, and myself – ther were namo.   *no others*
545   The MILLERE was a stout carl for the nones;
Ful byg he was of brawn, and eek of bones.   *muscle*
That proved wel, for over al ther he cam,
At wrastlynge he wolde have alwey the ram.
He was short-sholdred, brood, a thikke knarre;
550 Ther was no dore that he nolde heve of harre,
Or breke it at a rennyng with his heed.
His berd as any sowe or fox was reed,
And therto brood, as though it were a spade.
Upon the cop right of his nose he hade   *right on the tip*
555 A werte, and theron stood a toft of herys,
Reed as the brustles of a sowes erys;
His nosethirles blake were and wyde.   *nostrils*
A swerd and a bokeler bar he by his syde.
His mouth as greet was as a greet forneys.
560 He was a janglere and a goliardeys,
And that was moost of synne and harlotries.   *scurrility*
Wel koude he stelen corn and tollen thries;
And yet he hadde a thombe of gold, pardee.   *indeed*
A whit cote and a blew hood wered he.
565 A baggepipe wel koude he blowe and sowne,   *play*
And therwithal he broghte us out of towne.
    A gentil MAUNCIPLE was ther of a temple,
Of which achatours myghte take exemple   *buyers*
For to be wise in byynge of vitaille;   *shrewd; food*
570 For wheither that he payde or took by taille, *on credit*
Algate he wayted so in his achaat
That he was ay biforn and in good staat.

539–40 Honestly and in full, both on the wages he earned and on the increase
    of his flock.
545 An exceedingly strong fellow.
547 That was evident enough, for wherever he came.
548 A ram was the usual reward given to the winner of a wrestling match.
549 A thickset, sturdy fellow.
550 There was no door he was unwilling to heave off its hinges.
560 A loud talker and a coarse buffoon.
562 And take three times the legal toll on the corn he ground.
563 i.e. he was neither more nor less honest than other millers. (There is an
    allusion here to the old proverb 'An honest miller has a golden thumb,' which
    apparently means 'There are no honest millers.')
567 *gentil*, worthy; *Maunciple*, servant who bought provisions for an inn of
    court (*temple*).
571–2 At all times he was so cautious in his buying that he was always ahead
    of others and in an advantageous position.

Now is nat that of God a ful fair grace
That swich a lewed mannes wit shal pace   *ignorant; surpass*
575   The wisdom of an heep of lerned men?
Of maistres hadde he mo than thries ten,
That weren of lawe expert and curious,   *skilful*
Of which ther were a duszeyne in that hous
Worthy to been stywardes of rente and lond   *revenue*
580   Of any lord that is in Engelond,
To make hym lyve by his propre good   *on his own income*
In honour dettelees (but if he were   *unless he was mad*
      wood),
Or lyve as scarsly as hym list desire;
And able for to helpen al a shire
585   In any caas that myghte falle or happe;
And yet this Manciple sette hir aller cappe.
      The REVE was a sclendre colerik man.
His berd was shave as ny as ever he kan;   *shaven; close*
His heer was by his erys ful round yshorn;
590   His top was dokked lyk a preest biforn.
Ful longe were his legges and ful lene,
Ylyk a staf, ther was no calf ysene.   *like; visible*
Wel koude he kepe a gerner and a bynne;
Ther was noon auditour koude on him wynne.
595   Wel wiste he by the droghte and by the reyn   *knew*
The yeldynge of his seed and of his greyn.
His lordes sheep, his neet, his dayerye,   *cattle; dairy cows*
His swyn, his hors, his stoor, and his pultrye   *livestock*
Was hoolly in this Reves governynge,   *charge*
600   And by his covenant yaf the rekenynge,
Syn that his lord was twenty yeer of age.
Ther koude no man brynge hym in arrerage.
Ther nas baillif, ne hierde, nor oother   *herdsman*
      hyne,   *labourer*
That he ne knew his sleighte and his covyne;
605   They were adrad of hym as of the deeth.
His wonyng was ful faire upon an heeth;   *dwelling*
With grene trees yshadwed was his place.

576   i.e. he had more than thirty lawyers to provide for.
583   As economically as he pleases.
585   In any emergency that might arise.
586   Made fools of them all.
589–90   His hair was shorn all round above his ears; on top it was docked in
      front, like a priest's.
593   He could take good care of a granary or corn bin.
594   Who could get the better of him.
600   By the agreement he had with his lord he always rendered an account of
      the property entrusted to his charge.
602   No one could prove him to be in arrears.
604–5   Whose cunning and deceit were unknown to him; they were afraid of
      him as of death itself.

He koude bettre than his lord purchace.
Ful riche he was astored pryvely:
610 His lord wel koude he plesen subtilly,   *cunningly*
To yeve and lene hym of his owene good,
And have a thank, and yet a cote and hood.   *thanks*
In youthe he hadde lerned a good myster;   *trade*
He was a wel good wrighte, a carpenter.   *workman*
615 This Reve sat upon a ful good stot,   *farm horse*
That was al pomely grey and highte Scot.
A long surcote of pers upon he hade,
And by his syde he baar a rusty blade.
Of Northfolk was this Reve of which I telle,
620 Biside a toun men clepen Baldeswelle.
Tukked he was as is a frere aboute,
And evere he rood the hyndreste of oure   *hindmost*
        route.   *company*
    A SOMONOUR was ther with us in that place,
That hadde a fyr-reed cherubynnes face,
625 For saucefleem he was, with eyen narwe.   *pimply*
As hoot he was and lecherous as a sparwe,
With scalled browes blake and piled berd.   *scabby; scraggy*
Of his visage children were aferd.
Ther nas quyk-silver, lytarge, ne brymstoon,   *litharge*
630 Boras, ceruce, ne oille of tartre noon,   *borax; ceruse*
Ne oynement that wolde clense and byte,   *burn*
That hym myghte helpen of his whelkes white,   *pimples*
Nor of the knobbes sittynge on his chekes.
Wel loved he garleek, oynons, and eek lekes,
635 And for to drynken strong wyn, reed as blood;
Thanne wolde he speke and crie as he were wood.   *mad*
And whan that he wel dronken hadde the wyn,
Thanne wolde he speke no word but Latyn.
A fewe termes hadde he, two or thre,
640 That he had lerned out of som decree—
No wonder is, he herde it al the day;
And eek ye knowen wel how that a jay

609 He had secretly amassed a rich store of goods.
611 By giving and lending him his (i.e. the lord's) own goods.
616 That was all dapple-grey and called Scot.
617 He had on a long outer coat of blue-grey cloth.
620 Near a village called Bawdeswell (in Norfolk).
621 i.e. he shortened his coat by tucking it under his girdle in the manner of a
     friar.
623 The Summoner was a minor official employed to summon offenders before
     an ecclesiastical court, especially one presided over by an archdeacon.
624 Cherubim were usually painted with red faces by the medieval artist.
626 The sparrow was traditionally associated with lechery.
639–40 i.e. he had picked up two or three Latin tags in the court where he
     served.

Kan clepen 'Watte' as wel as kan the pope.   *Walter*
But whoso koude in oother thyng hym grope,
645   Thanne hadde he spent al his philosophie;
Ay '*Questio quid iuris*' wolde he crie.
He was a gentil harlot and a kynde;   *charming rascal*
A bettre felawe sholde men noght fynde.
He wolde suffre for a quart of wyn
650   A good felawe to have his concubyn
A twelf month, and excuse hym atte fulle;   *fully*
Ful prively a fynch eek koude he pulle.
And if he foond owher a good felawe,   *anywhere*
He wolde techen him to have noon awe   *fear*
655   In swich caas of the ercedekenes curs,
But if a mannes soule were in his purs;
For in his purs he sholde ypunysshed be.
'Purs is the ercedekenes helle,' seyde he.
But wel I woot he lyed right in dede;   *know*
660   Of cursyng oghte ech gilty man him drede,
For curs wol slee right as assoillyng savith,   *absolution*
And also war hym of a *Significavit*.
In daunger hadde he at his owene gise
The yonge girles of the diocise,
665   And knew hir conseil, and was al hir reed.
A gerland hadde he set upon his heed
As greet as it were for an ale-stake.
A bokeleer hadde he maad hym of a cake.   *loaf of bread*
With hym ther rood a gentil PARDONER   *noble*
670   Of Rouncivale, his freend and his compeer,   *companion*
That streight was comen from the court of Rome.
Ful loude he soong 'Com hider, love, to me!'

644 But if anyone knew how to test him further.
646 'The question is, what is the law on this point?'
652 i.e. on the quiet he indulged in illicit intercourse himself.
655 *In swich caas*, i.e. if he were caught in incontinence.
658 In other words, when the archdeacon threatens a sinner with hell, the real
      place of punishment for the victim will be his own purse.
660 Every guilty man ought to be afraid of excommunication.
662 *Significavit*, the first word of a writ for the imprisonment of an
      excommunicated person.
663–4 He had the young people of the diocese at his mercy, to do with as he
      pleased.
665 And knew their secrets, and was their adviser in everything.
667 *ale-stake*, support for the garland or bush which was the sign of a tavern.
669 *Pardoner*, an official whose true function was to convey papal indulgences
      (i.e. remissions of temporal punishment) to those who had received the
      sacrament of penance. According to canon law, he had no right to sell
      indulgences to all and sundry, as Chaucer's Pardoner is guilty of doing.
670 *Rouncivale*, the hospital and chapel of St Mary Roncevall, near Charing
      Cross in London.
672 Possibly a verse from some popular song of the time.

This Somonour bar to hym a stif burdoun;
Was nevere trompe of half so greet a soun. *trumpet; sound*
675 This Pardoner hadde heer as yelow as wex, *wax*
But smothe it heeng as dooth a strike of flex;
By ounces henge his lokkes that he hadde, *in thin clusters*
And therwith he his shuldres overspradde; *covered*
But thynne it lay, by colpons oon and oon. *in single shreds*
680 But hood, for jolitee, wered he noon, *fun; wore*
For it was trussed up in his walet.
Hym thoughte he rood al of the newe jet;
Dischevelee, save his cappe, he rood al bare.
Swiche glarynge eyen hadde he as an hare.
685 A vernycle hadde he sowed upon his cappe.
His walet, biforn hym in his lappe,
Bretful of pardoun, comen from Rome al hoot.
A voys he hadde as smal as hath a goot.
No berd hadde he, ne nevere sholde have;
690 As smothe it was as it were late shave. *lately shaven*
I trowe he were a geldyng or a mare.
But of his craft, from Berwyk into Ware, *at his trade*
Ne was ther swich another pardoner.
For in his male he hadde a pilwe-beer, *bag; pillow-case*
695 Which that he seyde was Oure Lady veyl:
He seyde he hadde a gobet of the seyl *piece*
That Seint Peter hadde, whan that he wente
Upon the see, til Jhesu Crist hym hente. *caught hold of*
He hadde a croys of latoun ful of stones,
700 And in a glas he hadde pigges bones.
But with thise relikes, whan that he fond *found*
A povre person dwellynge upon lond,
Upon a day he gat hym moore moneye
Than that the person gat in monthes tweye; *two*
705 And thus, with feyned flaterye and japes, *tricks*
He made the person and the peple his apes. *dupes*
But trewely to tellen atte laste,
He was in chirche a noble ecclesiaste.

673 Accompanied him with a powerful bass.
676 It hung down smoothly like a hank of flax.
682 He imagined he rode in the very latest fashion.
683 With his hair langing loose, he rode bareheaded except for his cap.
685 *vernycle*, miniature copy of St Veronica's sacred handkerchief, upon which
Christ's features were miraculously imprinted. This was the usual token
brought back by pilgrims to Rome, and the Pardoner no doubt wore one in
order to give the impression that he had lately come from Rome.
687 Brimful of indulgences.
692 From Berwick to Ware (in Hertfordshire), i.e. from the north to the south of
England.
699 A cross of brass, studded with false gems.
702 A poor parson living in the country.

Wel koude he rede a lessoun or a storie,
710 But alderbest he song an offertorie;
For wel he wiste, whan that song was songe,   *knew*
He moste preche and wel affile his tonge
To wynne silver, as he ful wel koude;   *knew how*
Therefore he song the murierly and loude.   *more pleasantly*
715   Now have I toold you soothly, in a clause,   *few words*
Th'estaat, th'array, the nombre, and eek   *rank; attire*
    the cause
Why that assembled was this compaignye
In Southwerk at this gentil hostelrye   *noble*
That highte the Tabard, faste by the Belle.
720 But now is tyme to yow for to telle
How that we baren us that ilke nyght,
Whan we were in that hostelrie alyght;
And after wol I telle of our viage   *journey*
And al the remenaunt of oure pilgrimage.   *rest*
725 But first I pray yow, of youre curteisye,
That ye n'arette it nat my vileynye,
Thogh that I pleynly speke in this mateere,
To telle yow hir wordes and hir cheere,   *behaviour*
Ne thogh I speke hir wordes proprely.   *exactly*
730 For this ye knowen al so wel as I,
Whoso shal telle a tale after a man,
He moot reherce as ny as evere he kan
Everich a word, if it be in his charge,
Al speke he never so rudeliche and large,
735 Or ellis he moot telle his tale untrewe,   *untruly*
Or feyne thyng, or fynde wordes newe.
He may nat spare, althogh he were his brother;
He moot as wel seye o word as another.
Crist spak hymself ful brode in hooly writ,   *plainly*
740 And wel ye woot no vileynye is it.
Eek Plato seith, whoso kan hym rede,
The wordes moote be cosyn to the dede.   *cousin*

709 *lessoun*, passage from Scripture read at divine service; *storie*, series of lessons
    from Scripture or from the life of a saint.
710 But best of all he sang an offertory. (This is the anthem usually sung while
    the people are making their offerings; but the Pardoner had found that he
    could persuade his congregation to give more generously by preaching them
    an eloquent sermon between the anthem and the collection.)
712 He had to preach and polish up his words.
719 That is called the Tabard, hard by the Bell (both Southwark inns).
721 What we did that same night.
726 That you do not attribute it to my bad manners.
731–4 Whoever tells a tale as someone else has told it must, if he has
    undertaken to do so, repeat every word as near as he can, however rudely and
    broadly he speaks.
738 He is bound to treat every word alike.
740 And you well know there is nothing coarse in what he says.

Also I prey yow to foryeve it me,
Al have I nat set folk in hir degree   *although*
745 Heere in this tale, as that they sholde stonde.
My wit is short, ye may wel understonde.
    Greet chiere made oure Hoost us everichon,   *good cheer*
And to the soper sette he us anon.
He served us with vitaille at the beste;
750 Strong was the wyn, and wel to drynke us leste.
A semely man OURE HOOSTE was withalle
For to been a marchal in an halle.
A large man he was with eyen stepe –   *prominent*
A fairer burgeys was ther noon in Chepe –
755 Boold of his speche, and wys, and wel ytaught,
And of manhod hym lakkede right naught.
Eek therto he was right a myrie man,
And after soper pleyen he bigan,   *to jest*
And spak of myrthe amonges othere thynges,
760 Whan that we hadde maad our rekenynges,   *paid*
And seyde thus: 'Now, lordynges, trewely,   *sirs*
Ye been to me right welcome, hertely;   *really*
For by my trouthe, if that I shal nat lye,
I saugh nat this yeer so myrie a compaignye   *saw*
765 Atones in this herberwe as is now.   *at one time; inn*
Fayn wolde I doon yow myrthe, wiste I how.
And of a myrthe I am right now bythoght,
To doon yow ese, and it shal coste noght.
    Ye goon to Caunterbury – God yow speede,
770 The blisful martir quite yow youre meede!   *reward you*
And wel I woot, as ye goon by the weye,
Ye shapen yow to talen and to pleye;
For trewely, confort ne myrthe is noon
To ride by the weye doumb as a stoon;
775 And therfore wol I maken yow disport,   *entertainment*
As I seyde erst, and doon yow som confort.   *before*
And if yow liketh alle by oon assent
For to stonden at my juggement,   *abide by*
And for to werken as I shal yow seye,   *do*
780 To-morwe, whan ye riden by the weye,
Now, by my fader soule that is deed,
But ye be myrie, I wol yeve yow myn heed!   *unless*
Hoold up youre hondes, withouten moore speche.'

---

750 It pleased us well to drink.
752 *marchal*, marshal, an official in a noble household who was responsible for
    the arrangement of banquets and ceremonies.
754 There is no better burgess in Cheapside.
766 I would gladly amuse you, if I knew how.
768 To give you pleasure, and it shall cost you nothing.
772 You intend to tell tales.
777 If you all with one accord find it agreeable.
783 *Hoold up youre hondes*, i.e. to signify assent.

Oure conseil was nat longe for to seche.	*opinion; seek*
785 Us thoughte it was noght worth to make it wys,	
And graunted hym withouten moore avys,	
And bad him seye his voirdit as hym leste.	
'Lordynges,' quod he, 'now herkneth for the beste;	
But taak it nought, I prey yow, in desdeyn.	
790 This is the poynt, to speken short and pleyn,	
That ech of yow, to shorte with oure weye,	
In this viage shal telle tales tweye	*two*
To Caunterbury-ward, I mene it so,	*towards Canterbury*
And homward he shal tellen othere two,	
795 Of aventures that whilom han bifalle.	
And which of yow that bereth hym best of	*acquits himself*
alle,	
That is to seyn, that telleth in this caas	
Tales of best sentence and moost solaas,	
Shal have a soper at oure aller cost	
800 Heere in this place, sittynge by this post,	
Whan that we come agayn fro Caunterbury.	
And for to make yow the moore mury,	
I wol myselven goodly with yow ryde,	*gladly*
Right at myn owene cost, and be youre gyde;	
805 And whoso wole my juggement withseye	*gainsay*
Shal paye al that we spenden by the weye.	
And if ye vouche sauf that it be so,	
Tel me anon, withouten wordes mo,	*more*
And I wol erly shape me therfore.'	
810 This thyng was graunted, and oure othes swore	*sworn*
With ful glad herte, and preyden hym also	*(we) begged*
That he wolde vouche sauf for to do so,	
And that he wolde been oure governour,	*ruler*
And of our tales juge and reportour,	*umpire*
815 And sette a soper at a certeyn pris,	
And we wol reuled been at his devys	*will*
In heigh and lough; and thus by oon assent	
We been acorded to his juggement.	
And therupon the wyn was fet anon;	
820 We dronken, and to reste wente echon,	
Withouten any lenger taryynge.	
Amorwe, whan that day bigan to sprynge,	*next morning*

---

785 It seemed to us it was not worth deliberating about.
787 Give whatever verdict he liked.
791 To shorten our journey with.
795 That have happened in the past.
797 *in this caas*, i.e. in the event of your doing this.
798 The most instructive and entertaining tales.
799 At the expense of us all.
809 And I will prepare for it without delay.
817 *In heigh and lough*, in high and low, i.e. in all things.

Up roos oure Hoost, and was oure aller cok,
And gadrede us togidre alle in a flok,
825 And forth we riden a litel moore than paas   *footpace*
Unto the wateryng of Seint Thomas;
And there oure Hoost bigan his hors areste   *stop*
And seyde, 'Lordynges, herkneth, if yow leste.   *please*
Ye woot youre foreward, and I it yow recorde.
830 If even-song and morwe-song accorde,
Lat se now who shal telle the firste tale.
As evere mote I drynke wyn or ale,
Whoso be rebel to my juggement
Shal paye for al that by the wey is spent.
835 Now draweth cut, er that we ferrer twynne;
He which that hath the shorteste shal bigynne.
Sire Kynyght,' quod he, 'my mayster and my lord,
Now draweth cut, for that is myn accord.   *agreement*
Cometh neer,' quod he, 'my lady Prioresse.
840 And ye, sire Clerk, lat be youre shamefastnesse,
Ne studieth noght; ley hond to, every man!'
Anon to drawen every wight bigan,   *person*
And shortly for to tellen as it was,
Were it by aventure, or sort, or cas,
845 The sothe is this, the cut fil to the Knyght,   *truth; fell*
Of which ful blithe and glad was every wyght,
And telle he moste his tale, as was resoun,   *right*
By foreward and by composicioun,   *agreement; compact*
As ye han herd; what nedeth wordes mo?   *more*
850 And whan this goode man saugh that it was so,
As he that wys was and obedient
To kepe his foreward by his free assent,
He seyde, 'Syn I shal bigynne the game,   *since*
What, welcome be the cut, a Goddes name!
855 Now lat us ryde, and herkneth what I seye.'
And with that word we ryden forth oure weye,
And he bigan with right a myrie cheere   *cheerfully*
His tale anon, and seyde as ye may heere.

*   *   *   *

823 Was cock for all of us, i.e. awoke us all.
826 A place for watering horses two miles from London on the pilgrims' way to Canterbury.
829 You know your agreement, and I remind you of it.
830 If evensong and matins agree, i.e. if you are still of the same mind this morning.
832 As I hope never to drink anything but wine or ale.
835 Now draw lots before we go any farther.
841 And stop your musing.
844 Whether it was by luck, or fate, or chance.
854 Why, let the draw be welcome, in God's name.

The Miller's Prologue

Heere folwen the wordes bitwene the
Hoost and the Millere

	WHAN that the Knyght had thus his tale ytoold,	
3110	In al the route nas ther yong ne oold	
	That he ne seyde it was a noble storie,	
	And worthy for to drawen to memorie;	*to be remembered*
	And namely the gentils everichon.	
	Oure Hooste lough and swoor, 'So moot I gon,	
3115	This gooth aright; unbokeled is the male.	
	Lat se now who shal telle another tale;	*let's see*
	For trewely the game is wel bigonne.	
	Now telleth ye, sir Monk, if that ye konne,	
	Somwhat to quite with the Knyghtes tale.'	*repay*
3120	The Millere, that for dronken was al pale,	
	So that unnethe upon his hors he sat,	*with difficulty*
	He nolde avalen neither hood ne hat,	*take off*
	Ne abyde no man for his curteisie,	
	But in Pilates voys he gan to crie,	
3125	And swoor, 'By armes, and by blood and bones,	*Christ's arms*
	I kan a noble tale for the nones,	*occasion*
	With which I wol now quite the Knyghtes tale.'	
	Oure Hooste saugh that he was dronke of ale,	
	And seyde, 'Abyd, Robyn, my leeve brother;	*dear*
3130	Som bettre man shal telle us first another.	
	Abyd, and lat us werken thriftily.'	*profitably*
	'By Goddes soule,' quod he, 'that wol nat I;	
	For I wol speke, or elles go my wey.'	
	Oure Hoost answerde, 'Tel on, a devel wey!	*in the devil's name*
3135	Thou art a fool; thy wit is overcome.'	
	'Now herkneth,' quod the Millere, 'alle and some!	*one and all*

3110–11 In all the company there was no one, young or old, who did not say.
3113 And especially all the gentlefolk.
3114–15 Our Host laughed and exclaimed, 'Upon my life, this is going well; the pack is opened (i.e. we have now sampled our wares).'
3120 Who was quite pale with drink.
3123 Nor had he the manners to wait for anyone else.
3124 A reference to the ranting Pilate of the mystery plays.

But first I make a protestacioun
That I am dronke, I knowe it by my soun;
And therfore if that I mysspeke or seye,   *speak wrongly*
3140 Wyte it the ale of Southwerk, I you preye.   *blame it on*
For I wol telle a legende and a lyf   *story*
Bothe of a carpenter and of his wyf,
How that a clerk hath set the wrightes cappe.'
     The Reve answerde and seyde, 'Stynt thy   *shut your row*
        clappe!
3145 Lat be thy lewed dronken harlotrye.
It is a synne and eek a greet folye
To apeyren any man, or hym defame,   *injure*
And eek to bryngen wyves in swich fame.
Thou mayst ynogh of othere thynges seyn.'
3150   This dronke Millere spak ful soone ageyn   *in reply*
And seyde, 'Leve brother Osewold,   *dear; Oswald*
Who hath no wyf, he is no cokewold.   *cuckold*
But I sey nat therfore that thou art oon;
Ther been ful goode wyves many oon,
3155 And evere a thousand goode ayeyns oon   *for every bad one*
        badde.
That knowestow wel thyself, but if thou   *unless you're mad*
        madde.
Why artow angry with my tale now?
I have a wyf, pardee, as wel as thow;   *indeed*
Yet nolde I, for the oxen in my plogh,
3160 Take upon me moore than ynogh,
As demen of myself that I were oon;
I wol bileve wel that I am noon.
An housbonde shal nat been inquisityf
Of Goddes pryvetee, nor of his wyf.   *secret purpose*
3165 So he may fynde Goddes foyson there,
Of the remenant nedeth nat enquere.'
     What sholde I moore seyn, but this Millere
He nolde his wordes for no man forbere,   *spare*
But told his cherles tale in his manere.   *churl's*

3138 By the sound of my own voice.
3143 How a student made a fool of the carpenter.
3145 Have done with your ignorant drunken ribaldry. (The Reeve's annoyance
   is explained by the fact that he is a carpenter himself by trade; see *General
   Prologue* 614.)
3148 And also to bring wives into disrepute.
3149 There are lots of other things for you to talk about.
3160–1 Presume to consider myself one (i.e. a cuckold).
3165 Provided he finds God's plenty there, i.e. provided his wife gives him all he
   wants.

3170   M'athynketh that I shal reherce it heere.
        And therfore every gentil wight I preye,   *person*
        For Goddes love, demeth nat that I seye
        Of yvel entente, but for I moot reherce
        Hir tales alle, be they bettre or werse,
3175   Or elles falsen som of my mateere.   *falsify*
        And therfore, whoso list it nat yheere,
        Turne over the leef and chese another tale;   *leaf; choose*
        For he shal fynde ynowe, grete and smale,   *enough*
        Of storial thyng that toucheth gentillesse,
3180   And eek moralitee and hoolynesse.   *also*
        Blameth nat me if that ye chese amys.   *wrongly*
        The Millere is a cherl, ye knowe wel this;
        So was the Reve eek and othere mo,
        And harlotrie they tolden bothe two.   *ribaldry*
3185   Avyseth yow, and put me out of blame;   *think well*
        And eek men shall nat maken ernest of game.

The Miller's Tale

Here bigynneth the Millere his Tale

        Whilom ther was dwellynge at Oxenford   *once*
        A riche gnof, that gestes heeld to bord,
        And of his craft he was a carpenter.
3190   With hym ther was dwellynge a poure scoler,
        Hadde lerned art, but al his fantasye   *fancy*
        Was turned for to lerne astrologye,
        And koude a certeyn of conclusiouns,
        To demen by interrogaciouns,
3195   If that men asked hym in certein houres

3170 I'm sorry to have to repeat it here.
3172–4 For the love of God, don't imagine I speak with any evil intention, but because I'm bound to tell all their tales.
3176–7 Anyone who doesn't wish to hear it.
3179 Of historical matter concerned with noble conduct.
3186 i.e. take a joke seriously.
3188 A well-off churl, who took in lodgers.
3190–1 A poor scholar who had studied the arts.
3193 ff. He knew a certain number of astrological operations for obtaining answers to questions concerning the future, including the state of the weather.

Whan that men sholde have droghte or elles shoures,
Or if men asked hym what sholde bifalle
Of every thyng; I may nat rekene hem alle.
    This clerk was cleped hende Nicholas.
3200 Of deerne love he koude and of solas;
And therto he was sleigh and ful privee,   *sly; secretive*
And lyk a mayden meke for to see.
A chambre hadde he in that hostelrye   *lodging-house*
Allone, withouten any compaignye.
3205 Ful fetisly ydight with herbes swoote;
And he hymself as sweete as is the roote
Of lycorys, or any cetewale.   *liquorice; ginger*
His Almageste, and bookes grete and smale,
His astrelabie, longynge for his art,
3210 His augrym stones layen faire apart,
On shelves couched at his beddes heed;   *placed*
His presse ycovered with a faldyng reed;
And al above ther lay a gay sautrie,   *psaltery*
On which he made a-nyghtes melodie
3215 So swetely that all the chambre rong;
And *Angelus ad virginem* he song;
And after that he song the Kynges Noote.
Ful often blessed was his myrie throte.
And thus this sweete clerk his tyme spente
3220 After his freendes fyndyng and his rente.
    This carpenter hadde wedded newe a wyf,   *newly*
Which that he lovede moore than his lyf;
Of eighteteene yeer she was of age.
Jalous he was, and heeld hire narwe in cage,   *closely*
3225 For she was wylde and yong, and he was old,
And demed hymself been lik a cokewold.

3199 This student was called gentle (pleasant, courteous) Nicholas.
3200 He knew all about secret love and consolation.
3202 As meek as a maiden to look at.
3205 Most handsomely decked with sweet-smelling herbs.
3208 *Almageste*, an astronomical treatise by Ptolemy, who lived at Alexandria
     in the second century A.D.
3209 His astrolabe, relating to his special skill.
3210 His counters (counting-stones) lay neatly apart.
3212 His cupboard covered with a red woollen cloth.
3216 *Angelus ad virginem*, the Angel to the virgin (a hymn on the
     Annunciation).
3217 *the Kynges Noote*, possibly the same as the medieval song called 'King
     William's Note.'
3220 On his friends' charity and his own income.
3226 And thought himself no better than a cuckold.

He knew nat Catoun, for his wit was rude,
That bad man sholde wedde his simylitude.
Men sholde wedden after hire estaat,
3230   For youthe and elde is often at debaat.   *variance*
But sith that he was fallen in the snare,   *since*
He moste endure, as oother folk, his care.   *sorrow*
        Fair was this yonge wyf, and therwithal
As any wezele hir body gent and smal.
3235   A ceynt she werede, barred al of silk,
A barmclooth as whit as morne milk
Upon hir lendes, ful of many a goore.
Whit was hir smok, and broyden al bifoore   *embroidered*
And eek bihynde, on hir coler aboute,
3240   Of col-blak silk, withinne and eek withoute.
The tapes of hir white voluper   *cap*
Were of the same suyte of hir coler;   *matched her collar*
Hir filet brood of silk, and set ful hye.
And sikerly she hadde a likerous ye;   *certainly; wanton eye*
3245   Ful smale ypulled were hire browes two,
And tho were bent and blake as any sloo.   *they; sloe*
She was ful moore blisful on to see
Than is the newe pere-jonette tree,
And softer than the wolle is of a wether.   *wool*
3250   And by hir girdel heeng a purs of lether,
Tasseled with silk, and perled with latoun.
In al this world, to seken up and doun,
There nys no man so wys that koude thenche   *imagine*
So gay a popelote or swich a wenche.   *poppet; such*
3255   Ful brighter was the shynyng of hir hewe
Than in the Tour the noble yforged newe.
But of hir song, it was as loude and yerne   *as for; eager*
As any swalwe sittynge on a berne.   *swallow; barn*

3227 He did not know Cato (the supposed author of a collection of Latin
      maxims studied in the grammar schools), for his mind was untutored.
3228 Who bade a man marry someone like himself.
3229 In keeping with their condition.
3234 Her body was as graceful and slender as a weasel's.
3235 She wore a girdle decorated with bars of silk.
3236-7 A gored apron, as white as morning milk, over her loins.
3239-40 All round her collar, with coal-black silk, inside and out.
3243 Her fillet was a broad band of silk, set high on her head.
3245 Her eyebrows were plucked to a narrow line.
3248 Than is the early pear-tree in new leaf.
3251 Studded with pearl-shaped knobs of brass.
3252 If you search high and low.
3255-6 She was brighter of complexion than a gold noble freshly minted in the
      Tower of London.

	Therto she koude skippe and make game,	*frolic*
3260	As any kyde or calf folwynge his dame.	*its*
	Hir mouth was sweete as bragot or the meeth,	
	Or hoord of apples leyd in hey or heeth.	*store; heather*
	Wynsynge she was, as is a joly colt,	
	Long as a mast, and upright as a bolt.	
3265	A brooch she baar upon hir lowe coler,	
	As brood as is the boos of a bokeler.	*boss; shield*
	Hir shoes were laced on hir legges hye.	
	She was a prymerole, a piggesnye,	
	For any lord to leggen in his bedde,	*lay*
3270	Or yet for any good yeman to wedde.	
	Now, sire, and eft, sire, so bifel the cas,	
	That on a day this hende Nicholas	
	Fil with this yonge wyf to rage and pleye,	*began; wanton*
	Whil that hir housbonde was at Oseneye,	
3275	As clerkes ben ful subtile and ful queynte;	*artful; sly*
	And prively he caughte hire by the queynte,	*stealthily*
	And seyde, 'Ywis, but if ich have my wille,	*unless I*
	For deerne love of thee, lemman, I spille.'	*perish*
	And heeld hire harde by the haunchebones,	
3280	And seyde, 'Lemman, love me al atones,	*sweetheart; at once*
	Or I wol dyen, also God me save!'	*so*
	And she sproong as a colt dooth in the trave,	
	And with hir heed she wryed faste awey,	*turned*
	And seyde, 'I wol nat kisse thee, by my fey!	*faith*
3285	Why, lat be,' quod she, 'lat be, Nicholas,	*stop it*
	Or I wol crie "out, harrow" and "allas!"	
	Do wey youre handes, for youre curteisye!'	
	This Nicholas gan mercy for to crye,	
	And spak so faire, and profred him so faste,	
3290	That she hir love hym graunted atte laste,	
	And swoor hir ooth, by seint Thomas of Kent,	
	That she wol been at his comandement,	
	Whan that she may hir leyser wel espie.	*opportunity*
	'Myn housbonde is so ful of jalousie	

3261 As bragget (a drink made of ale and honey) or mead.
3263 She was as frisky and skittish as a colt.
3264 Straight as a crossbow-bolt.
3268 She was a primrose, a pigsney (a term of endearment).
3270 *yeman*, yeoman, a servant of a superior grade, ranking between a squire and a page.
3274 *Oseneye*, Osney, near Oxford.
3282 *trave*, wooden frame for holding unruly horses while they are being shod.
3286 *out, harrow*, a cry for help.
3287 Be good enough to take your hands away.
3289 Spoke so civilly, and offered his services so eagerly.
3291 i.e. St Thomas Becket.

3295 That but ye wayte wel and been privee,	*watch; stealthy*
I woot right wel I nam but deed,' quod she.	
'Ye moste been ful deerne, as in this cas.'	*discreet*
'Nay, therof care thee noght,' quod Nicholas.	*worry*
'A clerk hadde litherly biset his whyle,	
3300 But if he koude a carpenter bigyle.'	
And thus they been accorded and ysworn	
To wayte a tyme, as I have told biforn.	
Whan Nicholas had doon thus everideel,	*done all this*
And thakked hire aboute the lendes weel,	*smacked*
3305 He kiste hire sweete and taketh his sawtrie,	
And pleyeth faste, and maketh melodie.	
Thanne fil it thus, that to the paryssh chirche,	*happened*
Cristes owene werkes for to wirche,	*do*
This goode wyf went on an haliday.	*religious festival*
3310 Hir forheed shoon as bright as any day,	
So was it wasshen whan she leet hir werk.	*left off*
Now was ther of that chirche a parissh clerk,	
The which that was ycleped Absolon.	*called*
Crul was his heer, and as the gold it shoon,	*curly*
3315 And strouted as a fanne large and brode;	
Ful streight and evene lay his joly shode.	*parting*
His rode was reed, his eyen greye as goos.	*complexion; goose*
With Poules wyndow corven on his shoos,	
In hoses rede he wente fetisly.	*elegantly*
3320 Yclad he was ful smal and properly	*finely; handsomely*
Al in a kirtel of a lyght waget;	*jacket; blue*
Ful faire and thikke been the poyntes set.	
And therupon he hadde a gay surplys	
As whit as is the blosme upon the rys.	*bough*
3325 A myrie child he was, so God me save.	*gay lad*
Wel koude he laten blood and clippe and shave,	
And maken a chartre of lond or acquitaunce.	*deed of release*
In twenty manere koude he trippe and daunce	*different ways*
After the scole of Oxenforde tho,	*at that time*
3330 And with his legges casten to and fro,	*fling*
And pleyen songes on a smal rubible;	*fiddle*
Therto he song som tyme a loud quynyble;	*falsetto*

3296 I know for certain it will be the death of me.
3299–3300 A student has made bad use of his time if he can't deceive a
     carpenter.
3312 *parissh clerk*, an official in minor orders who assisted the parish priest to
     perform the church services.
3315 And spread out as wide and broad as a fan (i.e. a basket used in
     winnowing grain).
3318 i.e. the leather uppers of his shoes were cut with designs resembling the
     tracery of a window in St Paul's.
3322 i.e. he had laces in profusion for fastening his jacket.
3326 He knew all about letting blood, cutting hair, and shaving.

And as wel koude he pleye on a giterne.	*guitar*
In al the toun nas brewhous ne taverne	
3335 That he ne visited with his solas,	*entertainment*
Ther any gaylard tappestere was.	*lively barmaid*
But sooth to seyn, he was somdeel	*somewhat*
squaymous	*squeamish*
Of fartyng, and of speche daungerous.	*fastidious*
This Absolon, that jolif was and gay,	*sprightly*
3340 Gooth with a sencer on the haliday,	*censer*
Sensynge the wyves of the parisshe faste;	*vigorously*
And many a lovely look on hem he caste,	
And namely on this carpenteris wyf.	*especially*
To looke on hire hym thoughte a myrie lyf,	*seemed to him*
3345 She was so propre and sweete and likerous.	*comely; wanton*
I dar wel seyn, if she hadde been a mous,	
And he a cat, he wolde hire hente anon.	*catch*
This parissh clerk, this joly Absolon,	
Hath in his herte swich a love-longynge	*passionate longing*
3350 That of no wyf took he noon offrynge;	*offering*
For curteisie, he seyde, he wolde noon.	*wanted none*
The moone, whan it was nyght, ful	
brighte shoon,	*brightly shone*
And Absolon his gyterne hath ytake,	
For paramours he thoghte for to wake.	
3355 And forth he gooth, jolif and amorous,	
Til he cam to the carpenteres hous	
A litel after cokkes hadde ycrowe,	
And dressed hym up by a shot-wyndowe	
That was upon the carpenteris wal.	
3360 He syngeth in his voys gentil and smal,	*thin*
'Now, deere lady, if thy wille be,	*if it please you*
I praye yow that ye wole rewe on me,'	*take pity*
Ful wel acordaunt to his gyternynge.	
This carpenter awook, and herde him synge,	
3365 And spak unto his wyf, and seyde anon,	
'What! Alison! herestow nat Absolon,	
That chaunteth thus under oure boures wal?'	*bedroom*
And she answerde hir housbonde therwithal,	
'Yis, God woot, John, I heere it every deel.'	*knows; all*
3370 This passeth forth; what wol ye bet than weel?	
Fro day to day this joly Absolon	
So woweth hire that hym is wo bigon.	
He waketh al the nyght and al the day;	
He kembeth his lokkes brode, and made hym gay;	*combs*

3354 For love's sake he resolved to stay awake.
3358 And took his stand near a casement window.
3363 To the tuneful accompaniment of his guitar.
3370 And so it went; what more do you want?
3372 Woos her so hard that he feels utterly miserable.

3375   He woweth hire by meenes and brocage,
        And swoor he wolde been hir owene page;
        He syngeth, brokkynge as a nyghtyngale;   *quavering*
        He sente hire pyment, meeth, and spiced ale,
        And wafres, pipyng hoot out of the   *wafer-cakes*
                gleede;   *embers*
3380   And, for she was of towne, he profred meede.
        For som folk wol ben wonnen for richesse,
        And somme for strokes, and somme for gentillesse.
            Somtyme, to shewe his lightnesse and   *agility*
                maistrye,   *great skill*
        He pleyeth Herodes upon a scaffold hye.
3384   But what availleth hym as in this cas?
        She loveth so this hende Nicholas
        That Absolon may blowe the bukkes horn;
        He ne hadde for his labour but a scorn.
        And thus she maketh Absolon hire ape,   *dupe*
3390   And al his ernest turneth til a jape.
        Ful sooth is this proverbe, it is no lye,   *very true; lie*
        Men seyn right thus, 'Alwey the nye slye
        Maketh the ferre leeve to be looth.'
        For though that Absolon be wood or wrooth,
3395   By cause that he fer was from hire sight,
        This nye Nicholas stood in his light.
            Now ber thee wel, thou hende Nicholas,   *do your best*
        For Absolon may waille and synge 'allas.'
        And so bifel it on a Saterday,
3400   This carpenter was goon til Osenay;
        And hende Nicholas and Alisoun
        Acorded been to this conclusioun,
        That Nicholas shal shapen hym a wyle   *hatch a plot*
        This sely jalous housbonde to bigyle;   *foolish*
3405   And if so be the game wente aright,
        She sholde slepen in his arm al nyght,
        For this was his desir and hire also.   *hers*
        And right anon, withouten wordes mo,   *more*

3375 With the help of go-betweens and agents.
3378 He sent her sweetened wine, mead.
3380 i.e. he offered her money because she lived in a town and so would have
      opportunities for spending it.
3381–2 Some people will be won by money, some by blows, and some by
      courtesy.
3384 He plays the part of Herod in a mystery play on a stage high above the
      ground.
3387 'To blow the buck's horn' means 'to work without reward.'
3390 And makes a joke of all his earnest efforts.
3392–3 'The sly one near at hand always makes the distant lover hateful.' (Cf.
      'out of sight, out of mind.')
3394–6 Mad though he was about it, Absalom was out of her sight, and so the
      handy Nicholas stood in his light.

This Nicholas no lenger wolde tarie,
3410 But dooth ful softe unto his chambre carie   *softly*
Bothe mete and drynke for a day or tweye,
And to hire housbonde bad hire for to seye,
If that he axed after Nicholas,
She sholde seye she nyste where he was,   *did not know*
3415 Of al that day she saugh hym nat with ye;   *during*
She trowed that he was in maladye,
For for no cry hir mayde koude hym calle,
He nolde answere for thyng that myghte falle.
   This passeth forth al thilke Saterday,   *goes on; that*
3420 That Nicholas stille in his chambre lay,   *quietly*
And eet and sleep, or dide what hym leste,   *he pleased*
Til Sonday, that the sonne gooth to reste.
This sely carpenter hath greet merveyle
Of Nicholas, or what thyng myghte hym eyle,   *ail*
3425 And seyde, 'I am adrad, by Seint Thomas,   *afraid*
It stondeth nat aright with Nicholas.
God shilde that he deyde sodeynly!
This world is now ful tikel, sikerly.   *unreliable; certainly*
I saugh to-day a cors yborn to chirche   *corpse; carried*
3430 That now, on Monday last, I saugh hym wirche.
   'Go up,' quod he unto his knave anoon,   *servant*
'Clepe at his dore, or knokke with a stoon.   *call*
Looke how it is, and tel me boldely.'
   This knave gooth hym up ful sturdily,
3435 And at the chambre dore whil that he stood,
He cride and knokked as that he were wood,   *mad*
'What! how! what do ye, maister Nicholay?
How may ye slepen al the longe day?'
But al for noghte, he herde nat a word.   *nothing*
3440 An hole he foond, ful lowe upon a bord,
Ther as the cat was wont in for to crepe,   *where*
And at that hole he looked in ful depe,
And at the laste he hadde of hym a sight.
This Nicholas sat evere capyng upright,
3445 As he had kiked on the newe moone.   *as if he had gazed*
Adoun he gooth, and tolde his maister soone   *down*
In what array he saugh this ilke man.
   This carpenter to blessen hym bigan,   *cross himself*

3416 She thought he must be ill.
3417–18 Her maid couldn't attract his attention for all her shouting; he just
    wouldn't answer at all.
3423–4 Wondered a great deal about Nicholas.
3426 All is not well with Nicholas.
3427 God forbid he should die suddenly.
3430 Of someone I saw working on Monday last.
3444 Sat staring straight up all the time.
3447 In what condition he had seen the man.

And seyde, 'Help us, seinte Frydeswyde!
3450 A man woot litel what hym shal bityde.   knows; happen
This man is falle, with his astromye,   astrology
In som woodnesse or in som agonye.   madness
I thoghte ay wel how that it sholde be!
Men sholde nat knowe of Goddes pryvetee.
3455 Ye, blessed be alwey a lewed man   ignorant
That noght but oonly his bileve kan!
So ferde another clerk with astromye;   fared
He walked in the feeldes, for to prye   peer
Upon the sterres, what ther sholde bifalle,
3460 Til he was in a marle-pit yfalle;   fallen
He saugh nat that. But yet, by seint Thomas,
Me reweth soore of hende Nicholas.
He shal be rated of his studiyng,   scolded for
If that I may, by Jhesus, hevene kyng!
3465 Get me a staf, that I may underspore,
Whil that thou, Robyn, hevest up the dore.
He shal out of his studiyng, as I gesse' –   leave off
And to the chambre dore he gan hym dresse.   went up
His knave was a strong carl for the nones,
3470 And by the haspe he haaf it of atones;   heaved
Into the floor the dore fil anon.   onto; fell
This Nicholas sat ay as stille as stoon,
And evere caped upward into the eir.
This carpenter wende he were in despeir,   supposed
3475 And hente hym by the sholdres myghtily,   seized
And shook hym harde, and cride spitously,   angrily
'What! Nicholay! what, how! what, looke adoun!
Awak, and thenk on Cristes passioun!
I crouche thee from elves and fro wightes.'
3480 Therwith the nyght-spel seyde he anon-rightes
On foure halves of the hous aboute,   sides
And on the thresshfold of the dore withoute: outside
'Jhesu Crist and seinte Benedight,   Benedict
Blesse this hous from every wikked wight,   creature
3485 For nyghtes verye, the white *pater-noster*!
Where wentestow, seinte Petres soster?'
          And atte laste this hende Nicholas
Gan for to sike soore, and seyde, 'Allas!   sigh

3456 Who knows nothing but his creed.
3459 To find out from them what was going to happen.
3462 I am very sorry for gentle Nicholas.
3465 So that I can push it under.
3469 See *General Prologue* 545.
3479 I will protect you with the sign of the cross from elves and other creatures.
3480 *nyght-spel*, charm recited at night to ward off evil spirits; *anon-rightes*,
     straightaway.
3485–6 The meaning of these lines is obscure.

Shal al the world be lost eftsoones now?'   *very soon*
3490   This carpenter answerde, 'What seystow?
What! thynk on God, as we doon, men that swynke.'   *labour*
    This Nicholas answerde, 'Fecche me drynke,
And after wol I speke in pryvetee   *private*
Of certeyn thyng that toucheth me and thee.   *concerns*
3495 I wol telle it noon oother man, certeyn.'
    This carpenter goth doun, and comth ageyn,   *back*
And broghte of myghty ale a large quart;
And whan that ech of hem had dronke his part,   *share*
This Nicholas his dore faste shette,   *shut*
3500 And doun the carpenter by hym he sette.
    He seyde 'John, myn hooste, lief and deere,   *beloved*
Thou shalt upon thy trouthe swere me heere   *honour*
That to no wight thou shalt this conseil wreye;
For it is Cristes conseil that I seye,
3505 And if thou telle it man, thou art forlore;   *damned*
For this vengeaunce thou shalt han therfore,   *for it*
That if thou wreye me, thou shalt be wood.'   *betray; mad*
'Nay, Crist forbede it, for his hooly blood!'   *forbid*
Quod tho this sely man, 'I nam no labbe;
3510 Ne, though I seye, I nam nat lief to gabbe.
Sey what thou wolt, I shal it nevere telle
To child ne wyf, by hym that harwed helle!'
    'Now John,' quod Nicholas, 'I wol nat lye;
I have yfounde in myn astrologye,
3515 As I have looked in the moone bright,   *gazed at*
That now a Monday next, at quarter nyght,
Shal falle a reyn, and that so wilde and wood,
That half so greet was nevere Noes flood.   *Noah's*
This world,' he seyde, 'in lasse than an hour
3520 Shal al be dreynt, so hidous is the   *overwhelmed; hideous*
        shour.
Thus shal mankynde drenche, and lese hir lyf.'   *drown; lose*
    This carpenter answerde, 'Allas, my wyf!
And shal she drenche? allas, myn Alisoun!'
For sorwe of this he fil almoost adoun,   *almost collapsed*
3525 And seyde, 'Is ther no remedie in this cas?'
    'Why, yis, for Gode,' quod hende Nicholas,   *by God*
'If thou wolt werken after loore and reed.

3500 And sat the carpenter down beside him.
3503 That you won't reveal this secret to a living soul.
3509–10 This simple man then said, 'I am no tell-tale; nor, though I say it
    myself, am I fond of idle gossip.'
3512 By Him who harrowed hell, i.e. Christ.
3516 On Monday next, when a quarter of the night is gone, i.e. at about 9 p.m.
3517 A deluge of rain shall fall, so wild and violent.
3527 If you will act on my instruction and advice.

Thou mayst nat werken after thyn   *on your own account*
    owene heed;
For thus seith Salomon, that was ful trewe,
3530 "Werk al by conseil, and thou shalt nat rewe."
And if thou werken wolt by good conseil,
I undertake, withouten mast and seyl,
Yet shal I saven hire and thee and me.
    Hastow nat herd hou saved was Noe,
3535 Whan that oure Lord hadde warned hym biforn   *beforehand*
That al the world with water sholde be lorn?'   *destroyed by*
    'Yis,' quod this Carpenter, 'ful yoore ago.'   *long, long ago*
    'Hastou nat herd,' quod Nicholas, 'also
The sorwe of Noe with his felaweshipe,
3540 Er that he myghte gete his wyf to shipe?   *on board*
Hym hadde be levere, I dar wel undertake,
At thilke tyme, than alle his wetheres blake
That she hadde had a ship hirself allone.
And therfore, woostou what is best to doone?
3545 This asketh haste, and of an hastif thyng   *urgent*
Men may nat preche or maken tariyng.   *delay*
    Anon go gete us faste into this in
A knedyng-trogh, or ellis a kymelyn,
For ech of us, but looke that they be large,   *see*
3550 In which we mowe swymme as in a barge,
And han therinne vitaille suffisant   *food*
But for a day, – fy on the remenant!
The water shal aslake and goon away   *grow less*
Aboute pryme upon the nexte day.
3555 But Robyn may nat wite of this, thy knave,   *know; servant*
Ne eek thy mayde Gille I may nat save;
Axe nat why, for though thou aske me,
I wol nat tellen Goddes pryvetee.   *secret purpose*
Suffiseth thee, but if thy wittes madde,
3560 To han as greet a grace as Noe hadde.   *have*

3530 'Do all things by advice, and you shall not regret it.' (See Ecclus. xxxii. 19.)
3539 ff. The trouble Noah had to persuade his wife to go on board the Ark is one of the main comic episodes of the play of Noah in most of the English cycles of mystery plays.
3541–3 I dare say he would have given all his black wethers for her to have had a ship to herself on that occasion.
3544 Do you know what is the best thing to do?
3547 Go and quickly fetch into the house.
3548 A kneading-trough, or else a shallow tub (used for brewing).
3550 In which we can float as in a ship.
3552 Never mind the rest (i.e. don't worry about food for the following days).
3554 *pryme*, 9 a.m.
3559 You should be satisfied, unless you're mad.

Thy wyf shal I wel saven, out of doute.
Go now thy wey, and speed thee heer-aboute.   *hurry up about it*
    But whan thou hast, for hire and thee and me,
Ygeten us thise knedyng-tubbes thre,   *got*
3565 Thanne shaltow hange hem in the roof ful hye,
That no man of oure purveiaunce espye.
And whan thou thus hast doon, as I have seyd,
And hast oure vitaille faire in hem yleyd,   *properly; laid*
And eek an ax, to smyte the corde atwo,
3570 Whan that the water comth, that we may go,
And breke an hole an heigh, upon the gable,
Unto the gardyn-ward, over the stable,
That we may frely passen forth oure way,
Whan that the grete shour is goon away,
3575 Thanne shaltou swymme as myrie, I undertake,   *merrily*
As dooth the white doke after hire drake.   *duck*
Thanne wol I clepe, 'How, Alison! how, John!
Be myrie, for the flood wol passe anon.'
And thou wolt seyn, 'Hayl, maister Nicholay!
3580 Good morwe, I se thee wel, for it is day.'
And thanne shul we be lordes al oure lyf
Of al the world, as Noe and his wyf.
    But of o thyng I warne thee ful right: *straight*
Be wel avysed on that ilke nyght   *very careful*
3585 That we ben entred into shippes bord,
That noon of us ne speke nat a word,
Ne clepe, ne crie, but be in his preyere;
For it is Goddes owene heeste deere.   *command*
    Thy wyf and thou moote hange fer atwynne;   *far apart*
3590 For that bitwixe yow shal be no synne,
Namoore in lookyng than ther shal in deede.
This ordinance is seyd. Go, God thee speede!   *rule is made*
Tomorwe at nyght, whan men ben alle aslepe,
Into oure knedyng-tubbes wol we crepe,
3595 And sitten there, abidyng Goddes grace.
Go now thy wey, I have no lenger space   *time*
To make of this no lenger sermonyng.
Men seyn thus, 'sende the wise, and sey no thyng:'
Thou art so wys, it needeth thee nat teche.
3600 Go, save oure lyf, and that I the biseche.'

3561 Your wife I shall certainly save, never fear.
3566 So that no one can see what provision we have made for ourselves.
3571 And break a hole high up in the gable.
3572 Facing the garden, above the stable.
3587 Call or cry out, or do anything but pray.
3590 So that there shall be no sinful conduct between you.
3597 To speak of this at greater length.
3598 i.e. 'a word to the wise.'

This sely carpenter goth forth his wey.   *simple*
Ful ofte he seide 'allas' and 'weylawey,'
And to his wyf he tolde his pryvetee,   *secret*
And she was war, and knew it bet than he,   *aware; better*
3605 What al this queynte cast was for to seye.
But nathelees she ferde as she wolde deye,
And seyde, 'Allas! go forth thy wey anon,
Help us to scape, or we been dede echon!   *escape*
I am thy trewe, verray wedded wyf;   *faithful*
3610 Go, deere spouse, and help to save oure lyf.'
Lo, which a greet thyng is affeccioun!
Men may dyen of ymaginacioun,
So depe may impressioun be take.
This sely carpenter bigynneth quake;   *tremble*
3615 Hym thynketh verraily that he may see
Noees flood come walwynge as the see   *rolling*
To drenchen Alisoun, his hony deere.
He wepeth, weyleth, maketh sory cheere;
He siketh with ful many a sory swogh;
3620 He gooth and geteth hym a knedyng-trogh,
And after that a tubbe and a kymelyn,
And pryvely he sente hem to his in,
And heng hem in the roof in pryvetee.   *hung*
His owene hand he made laddres thre,   *with his own hand*
3625 To clymben by the ronges and the stalkes   *rungs; uprights*
Unto the tubbes hangynge in the balkes,   *beams*
And hem vitailled, bothe trogh and tubbe,   *provisioned*
With breed and chese, and good ale in a jubbe,   *jug*
Suffisynge right ynogh as for a day.
3630 But er that he hadde maad al this array,   *preparation*
He sente his knave, and eek his wenche also,   *maid*
Upon his nede to London for to go.
And on the Monday, whan it drow to nyght,   *drew near*
He shette his dore withoute candel-lyght,
3635 And dressed alle thyng as it sholde be.   *made ready*
And shortly, up they clomben alle thre;   *climbed*
They seten stille wel a furlong way.
'Now, *Pater-noster*, clom!' seyde Nicholay.
And 'clom,' quod John, and 'clom,' seyde Alisoun.
3640 This carpenter seyde his devocioun,

3605 What all this curious scheming meant.
3606 Nevertheless she behaved like someone in danger of death.
3611 What a strong thing feeling is!
3613 So deep an impression may be made by it.
3615 It seems to him he can really see.
3618–19 He weeps, wails, and glooms; he heaves many a sad sigh.
3632 To London to attend to some business for him.
3637 They sat still for a short while.
3638 *clom*, mum, be quiet.

	And stille he sit, and biddeth his preyere,	*sits; says*
	Awaitynge on the reyn, if he it heere.	
	The dede sleep, for wery bisynesse,	
	Fil on this carpenter right, as I gesse,	*fell*
3645	Aboute corfew-tyme, or litel moore;	
	For travaille of his goost he groneth soore	
	And eft he routeth, for his heed myslay.	
	Doun of the laddre stalketh Nicholay,	*from; creeps*
	And Alisoun ful softe adoun she spedde;	*hurried down*
3650	Withouten wordes mo they goon to bedde,	
	Ther as the carpenter is wont to lye.	*where*
	Ther was the revel and the melodye;	*revelry*
	And thus lith Alison and Nicholas,	*lie*
	In bisynesse of myrthe and of solas,	
3655	Til that the belle of laudes gan to rynge,	
	And freres in the chauncel gonne synge.	
	This parissh clerk, this amorous Absolon,	
	That is for love alwey so wo bigon,	
	Upon the Monday was at Oseneye	
3660	With compaignye, hym to disporte and pleye,	*amuse himself*
	And axed upon cas a cloisterer	
	Ful prively after John the carpenter;	*in strict confidence*
	And he drough hym apart out of the chirche,	*drew; aside*
	And seyde, 'I noot, I saugh hym heere nat wirche	
3665	Syn Saterday; I trowe that he be went	
	For tymber, ther oure abbot hath hym sent;	*to where*
	For he is wont for tymber for to go,	
	And dwellen at the grange a day or two;	
	Or elles he is at his hous, certeyn.	
3670	Where that he be, I kan nat soothly seyn.'	*truly*
	This Absolon ful joly was and light,	*light-hearted*
	And thoghte, 'Now is tyme to wake al nyght;	*stay awake*
	For sikirly I saugh hym nat stirynge	*certainly*
	Aboute his dore, syn day bigan to sprynge.	
3675	So moot I thryve, I shal, at cokkes crowe,	
	Ful pryvely knokken at his wyndowe	*stealthily*

3642 Watching and listening for the rain.
3643 Brought on by his exhausting work.
3645 *corfew-tyme*, about 8 p.m.
3646–7 Disturbed in spirit, he groans loudly, and then he snores, for his head
    lay askew.
3654 Engaged in pleasant, entertaining work.
3655 *laudes*, lauds, the service following matins and usually sung at daybreak.
3661 Asked by chance a cloisterer (i.e. monk).
3664–5 I don't know, I haven't seen him working here since Saturday; I think
    he has gone.
3668 *grange*, granary (one belonging to a religious house is meant here).
3673–4 For certainly I haven't seen him stir outside his house since day began.
3675 As I hope to prosper.

That stant ful lowe upon his boures wal.
To Alison now wol I tellen al
My love-longynge, for yet I shal nat mysse   *fail*
3680 That at the leeste wey I shal hire kisse.
Som maner confort shal I have, parfay.   *upon my word*
My mouth hath icched al this longe day;   *itched*
That is a signe of kissyng atte leeste.
Al nyght me mette eek I was at a feeste.   *I dreamt also*
3685 Therfore I wol go slepe an houre or tweye,
And al the nyght thanne wol I wake and pleye.'
    Whan that the firste cok hath crowe, anon
Up rist this joly lovere Absolon,   *gets*
And hym arraieth gay, at poynt-devys.
3690 But first he cheweth greyn and   *cardamom*
        lycorys.   *liquorice*
To smellen sweete, er he hadde kembd his heer.   *combed; hair*
Under his tonge a trewe-love he beer,
For therby wende he to ben gracious.
He rometh to the carpenteres hous,   *makes his way*
3695 And stille he stant under the shot-wyndowe –
Unto his brest it raughte, it was so lowe –   *reached*
And softe he cougheth with a semy soun: *gentle sound*
'What do ye, hony-comb, sweete Alisoun,
My faire bryd, my sweete cynamome?   *bird; cinnamon*
3700 Awaketh, lemman myn, and speketh to me!   *beloved*
Wel litel thynken ye upon my wo,
That for youre love I swete ther I go.
No wonder is thogh that I swelte and swete;   *swoon*
I moorne as dooth a lamb after the tete.   *mourn; teat*
3705 Ywis, lemman, I have swich love-longynge,
That lik a turtel trewe is my moornynge.   *turtle-dove*
I may nat ete na moore than a mayde.'   *eat*
    'Go fro the wyndow, Jakke fool,' she sayde;
'As help me God, it wol nat be "com pa me."
3710 I love another – and elles I were to blame –
Wel bet than thee, by Jhesu, Absolon.
Go forth thy wey, or I wol caste a ston,
And lat me slepe, a twenty devel wey!'   *in the devil's name*
    'Allas,' quod Absolon, 'and weylawey,
3715 That trewe love was evere so yvel biset!'   *badly used*

3677 That is set low in the wall of his bedroom.
3689 And dresses himself in gay clothes, with every care.
3692–3 He carried a leaf of herb paris under his tongue, for he thought in this
    way to make himself agreeable.
3701–2 You give little thought to my sorrow, and how I sweat for love of you
    wherever I walk.
3708 *Jakke*, Jack (here used derisively).
3709 It won't be a case of 'come kiss me,' i.e. you won't get a kiss from me. (The
    words *com pa me* may be from a popular song of the time.)

Thanne kysse me, syn it may be no bet,
For Jhesus love, and for the love of me.'
   'Wiltow thanne go thy wey therwith?' quod she.
   'Ye, certes, lemman,' quod this Absolon.
3720   'Thanne make thee redy,' quod she, 'I come anon.'
And unto Nicholas she seyde stille,   *softly*
'Now hust, and thou shalt laughen al thy fille.'   *hush*
   This Absolon doun sette hym on his knees   *knelt down*
And seyde, 'I am a lord at alle degrees;
3725 For after this I hope ther cometh moore.
Lemman, thy grace, and sweete bryd, thyn oore!'
   The wyndow she undoth, and that in haste.
'Have do,' quod she, 'com of, and speed the faste,
Lest that oure neighebores thee espie.'
3730   This Absolon gan wype his mouth ful drie.
Derk was the nyght as pich, or as the cole,   *pitch; coal*
And at the wyndow out she putte hir hole,
And Absolon, hym fil no bet ne wers,
But with his mouth he kiste hir naked ers
3735 Ful savourly, er he were war of this.   *enjoyably*
Abak he stirte, and thoughte it was amys,
For wel he wiste a womman hath no berd.
He felte a thyng al rough and long yherd,   *haired*
And seyde, 'Fy! allas! what have I do?'   *done*
3740   'Tehee!' quod she, and clapte the wyndow to,
And Absolon gooth forth a sory pas.   *miserably*
   'A berd! a berd!' quod hende Nicholas,
'By Goddes corpus, this goth faire and weel.'
   This sely Absolon herde every deel,   *wretched; everything*
3745 And on his lippe he gan for anger byte,
And to hymself he seyde, 'I shal thee quyte.'   *pay you back*
   Who rubbeth now, who froteth now his lippes   *chafes*
With dust, with sond, with straw, with clooth,
      with chippes,   *shavings*
But Absolon, that seith ful ofte, 'Allas!
3750 My soule bitake I unto Sathanas,   *commend*
But me were levere than al this toun,' quod he,
'Of this despit awroken for to be.
Allas,' quod he, 'allas, I ne hadde ybleynt!'
His hoote love was coold and al yqueynt;   *quenched*

3716 Since there's no hope of anything better.
3718 Will you go away when you've had it?
3724 I'm happy as a lord of high degree.
3726 Thy grace, beloved, and favour, my sweet bird.
3728 Have done . . . come along and be quick about it.
3733 Nothing better nor worse happened to him.
3736 He started back, and thought something was wrong.
3751-2 I would rather be revenged for this insult than own all this town.
3753 Alas, that I didn't turn aside.

3755 For fro that tyme that he hadde kist hir ers,	*from*
Of paramours he sette nat a kers;	
For he was heeled of his maladie.	*cured*
Ful ofte paramours he gan deffie,	
And weep as dooth a child that is ybete.	*wept; beaten*
3760 A softe paas he wente over the strete	
Until a smyth men cleped daun Gerveys,	
That in his forge smythed plough harneys;	*made; fittings*
He sharpeth shaar and kultour bisily.	*share; coulter*
This Absolon knokketh al esily,	*gently*
3765 And seyde, 'Undo, Gerveys, and that anon.'	
'What, who artow?' 'It am I, Absolon.'	
'What, Absolon! for Cristes sweete tree,	*cross*
Why rise ye so rathe? ey, *benedicitee!*	*early; bless me*
What eyleth yow? Som gay gerl, God it woot,	*ails; knows*
3770 Hath broght yow thus upon the viritoot.	
By seinte Note, ye woot wel what I mene.'	*Neot*
This Absolon ne roghte nat a bene	
Of all his pley; no word agayn he yaf;	
He hadde moore tow on his distaf	
3775 Than Gerveys knew, and seyde, 'Freend so deere,	
That hoote kultour in the chymenee heere,	
As lene it me, I have therwith to doone,	
And I wol brynge it thee agayn ful soone.'	
Gerveys answerde, 'Certes, were it gold,	
3780 Or in a poke nobles alle untold,	
Thou sholdest have, as I am trewe smyth.	
Ey, Cristes foo! what wol ye do therwith?'	*foe*
'Therof,' quod Absolon, 'be as be may.	
I shal wel telle it thee to-morwe day' –	
3785 And caughte the kultour by the colde stele.	*handle*
For softe out at the dore he gan to stele,	*softly; stole*
And wente unto the carpenteris wal.	
He cogheth first, and knokketh therwithal	*coughs*
Upon the wyndowe, right as he dide er.	*before*
3790 This Alison answerde, 'Who is ther	
That knokketh so? I warante it a theef.'	
'Why, nay,' quod he, 'God woot, my sweete leef,	*beloved*

3756 He didn't care a damn (lit. cress) for wenches.
3758 Many a time he renounced all earthly love.
3760–1 He crept quietly across the street to a blacksmith called master Gervais.
3770 *upon the viritoot*, astir, on the trot.
3772–3 Didn't think much of (lit. care a bean for) his joke; he said nothing in reply.
3774 i.e. had other business on hand.
3777 Please lend it me; there's something I have to do with it.
3780 Or an untold number of gold nobles in a bag.
3784 I shall tell you all about it tomorrow.

I am thyn Absolon, my deerelyng.
Of gold,' quod he, 'I have thee broght a ryng.
3795 My mooder yaf it me, so God me save;
Ful fyn it is, and therto wel ygrave.'   *engraved*
This wol I yeve thee, if thou me kisse.'
      This Nicholas was risen for to pisse,
And thoughte he wolde amenden al the jape;
3800 He sholde kisse his ers er that he scape.   *got away*
And up the wyndowe dide he hastily,
And out his ers he putteth pryvely   *stealthily*
Over the buttok, to the haunche-bon;
And therwith spak this clerk, this Absolon,
3805 'Spek, sweete bryd, I noot nat where thou art.'
      This Nicholas anon leet fle a fart,   *let fly*
As greet as it had been a thonder-dent,   *clap of thunder*
That with the strook he was almoost yblent;
And he was redy with his iren hoot,
3810 And Nicholas amydde the ers he smoot.   *in the middle of*
      Of gooth the skyn an hande-brede aboute,
The hoote kultour brende so his toute,   *backside*
And for the smert he wende for to dye.
As he were wood, for wo he gan to crye,
3815 'Help! water! water! help, for Goddes herte!'
      This carpenter out of his slomber sterte,   *started*
And herde oon crien 'water' as he were wood,   *someone*
And thoughte, 'Allas, now comth Nowelis flood!'
He sit hym up withouten wordes mo,
3820 And with his ax he smoot the corde atwo,
And doun gooth al; he foond neither to selle,
Ne breed ne ale, til he cam to the celle
Upon the floor, and ther aswowne he lay.   *in a swoon*
      Up stirte hire Alison and Nicholay,   *jumped*
3825 And criden 'out' and 'harrow' in the strete.
The neighebores, bothe smale and grete,
In ronnen for to gauren on this man,   *ran; stare at*
That yet aswowne lay, bothe pale and wan,
For with the fal he brosten hadde his arm.   *broken*

3799 Improve on the joke.
3800 *He*, i.e. Absalom.
3803 Past the buttocks.
3808 So that he (i.e. Absalom) was almost blinded by the blast.
3811 A handsbreadth all round.
3813 He thought he would die with the pain of it.
3818 *Nowelis*, Noah's. (The illiterate carpenter has confused *Noe* 'Noah' and *Nowel* 'Christmas.')
3819–20 He sits up and without more ado he cuts the rope in two with his axe.
3821–3 He found neither bread nor ale for sale (i.e. he found nothing to stop him) till he reached the floor-boards.
3825 *out, harrow*, cries for help.

3830	But stonde he moste unto his owene harm;	
	For whan he spak, he was anon bore doun	*talked down*
	With hende Nicholas and Alisoun.	*by*
	They tolden every man that he was wood,	*mad*
	He was agast so of Nowelis flood	*terrified*
3835	Thurgh fantasie, that of his vanytee	
	He hadde yboght hym knedyng-tubbes thre,	
	And hadde hem hanged in the roof above;	
	And that he preyed hem, for Goddes love,	
	To sitten in the roof, *par compaignye.*	*for company*
3840	The folk gan laughen at his fantasye;	*laughed*
	Into the roof they kiken and they cape,	*peep; gape*
	And turned al his harm unto a jape.	
	For what so that this carpenter answerde,	*whatever*
	It was for noght, no man his reson herde.	
3845	With othes grete he was so sworn adoun	
	That he was holde wood in al the toun;	*considered mad*
	For every clerk anonright heeld with oother.	
	They seyde, 'The man is wood, my leeve brother';	
	And every wight gan laughen at this stryf.	*commotion*
3850	Thus swyved was this carpenteris wyf,	*copulated with*
	For al his kepyng and his jalousye;	
	And Absolon hath kist hir nether ye;	*eye*
	And Nicholas is scalded in the towte.	
	This tale is doon, and God save al the rowte!	*company*

Heere endeth the Millere his Tale

3830 He had to put up with his injury.
3835–6 In his imagination, that he had been foolish enough to buy himself three kneading-tubs.
3842 And made a joke of all his suffering.
3844 It was in vain, for no one listened to what he said.
3847 i.e. every student immediately took Nicholas's part.

The Reeve's Prologue

The Prologe of the Reves Tale

3855	WHAN folk hadde laughen at this nyce cas	*ludicrous affair*
	Of Absolon and hende Nicholas,	
	Diverse folk diversely they seyde,	
	But for the moore part they loughe and pleyde.	
	Ne at this tale I saugh no man hym gréve,	*get angry*
3860	But it were oonly Osewold the Reve.	*except*
	By cause he was of carpenteris craft,	
	A litel ire is in his herte ylaft;	*left*
	He gan to grucche, and blamed it a lite.	*grumble; little*
	'So theek,' quod he, 'ful wel koude I thee quite	
3865	With bleryng of a proud milleres ye,	
	If that me liste speke of ribaudye.	
	But ik am oold, me list not pley for age;	
	Gras tyme is doon, my fodder is now forage;	
	This white top writeth myne olde yeris;	
3870	Myn herte is also mowled as myne heris,	
	But if I fare as dooth an open-ers,—	
	That ilke fruyt is ever lenger the wers,	
	Til it be roten in mullok or in stree.	
	We olde men, I drede, so fare we:	*I'm afraid*
3875	Til we be roten, kan we nat be rype;	
	We hoppen alwey whil that the world wol pype.	
	For in ouer wyl ther stiketh evere a nayl,	
	To have an hoor heed and a grene tayl,	*hoary; tail*
	As hath a leek; for thogh oure myght be goon,	*strength*
3880	Oure wyl desireth folie evere in oon.	

3857 Different people expressed different opinions of the tale.
3858 But for the most part they laughed and joked about it.
3864–6 As I hope to prosper . . . I could pay you back in full with a story of the hoodwinking of a proud miller, if I chose to tell a ribald tale.
3867 But I am old; I'm past the age for fun.
3868 My grazing time is over, I now feed on hay (as horses do in winter).
3869 These white hairs announce my age.
3870 My heart is grown as mouldy as my hair.
3871–3 Unless I'm like a medlar, which goes from bad to worse, until at last it rots in straw or on a rubbish-heap. (The fruit of the medlar-tree is eaten when it has decayed.)
3876 We dance as long as the world will pipe for us. (See Matt. xi.17.)
3877 For there is always this hindrance to our desire.
3880 We go on hankering after folly.

For whan we may nat doon, than wol we speke;
Yet in oure asshen olde is fyr yreke.
   Foure gleedes han we, which I shal devyse,—   *embers; mention*
Avauntyng, liying, anger, coveitise;   *boasting; covetousness*
3885 Thise foure sparkles longen unto eelde.
Oure olde lemes mowe wel been unweelde,
But wyl ne shal nat faillen, that is sooth.   *desire; truth*
And yet ik have alwey a coltes tooth,
As many a yeer as it is passed henne
3890 Syn that my tappe of lif bigan to renne.   *since; run*
For sikerly, whan I was bore, anon
Deeth drough the tappe of lyf and leet it gon;
And ever sithe hath so the tappe yronne
Til that almoost al empty is the tonne.   *cask*
3895 The streem of lyf now droppeth on the chymbe.
The sely tonge may wel rynge and chymbe   *foolish; chime*
Of wrecchednesse that passed is ful yoore;   *long ago*
With olde folk, save dotage, is namoore!'
   What that oure Hoost hadde herd this sermonyng,
3900 He gan to speke as lordly as a kyng.
He seide, 'What amounteth al this wit?
What shul we speke alday of hooly writ?
What devel made a reve for to preche,
Or of a soutere a shipman or a leche.   *cobbler; physician*
3905 Sey forth thy tale, and tarie nat the tyme;   *waste*
Lo Depeford! and it is half-wey pryme.
Lo Grenewych, ther many a shrewe is inne!
It were al tyme thy tale to bigynne.'   *quite*
   'Now, sires,' quod this Osewold the Reve,
3910 'I pray yow alle that ye nat yow greve,
Thogh I answere, and somdeel sette his howve;
For leveful is with force force of-showve.

3882 Still, in our old ashes, there is fire raked together.
3885 These four small sparks belong to old age.
3886 Our old limbs may well be feeble.
3888 *a coltes tooth*, one of the first set of teeth of a horse, and hence 'youthful or wanton desires.'
3889 In spite of the many years that have passed.
3891–2 For certainly, when I was born, death at once turned on the tap of life and let it run.
3895 Now drips on to the rim (of the cask), i.e. no longer flows out in a steady stream.
3898 There is nothing left for old folk but their dotage.
3901 What does all this wisdom amount to?
3902 Why must we always speak of holy writ?
3906 *half-wey pryme*, midway between 6 and 9 a.m.
3907 There's Greenwich, where many a rascal lives.
3911 And make a bit of a fool of him (i.e. the Miller).
3912 For it is allowable to repel force by force.

This dronke Millere hath ytoold us heer
How that bigyled was a carpenteer,
3915 Peraventure in scorn, for I am oon.   *perhaps*
And, by youre leve, I shal hym quite anoon;   *pay him back*
Right in his cherles termes wol I speke.
I pray to God his nekke mote to-breke;   *may break*
He kan wel in myn eye seen a stalke,·   *piece of straw*
3920 But in his owene he kan nat seen a balke.'   *beam*

The Reeve's Tale

Heere bigynneth the Reves Tale

AT TRUMPYNGTOUN, nat fer fro Cantebrigge,   *Cambridge*
Ther gooth a brook, and over that a brigge,   *runs*
Upon the whiche brook ther stant a melle;   *stands; mill*
And this is verray sooth that I yow telle.   *exact truth*
3925 A millere was ther dwellynge many a day;
As any pecok he was proud and gay.
Pipen he koude and fisshe, and nettes beete,
And turne coppes, and wel wrastle and sheete;
Ay by his belt he baar a long panade,
3930 And of a swerd ful trenchant was the blade.   *sword; sharp*
A joly poppere baar he in his pouche;   *handsome dagger*
Ther was no man, for peril, dorste hym touche.
A Sheffeld thwitel baar he in his hose.   *Sheffield knife*
Round was his face, and camus was his nose;   *flat*
3935 As piled as an ape was his skulle.   *bald*
He was a market-betere atte fulle.
Ther dorste no wight hand upon hym legge,

3917 I shall use just the same low language as he has done.
3919–20 See Matt. vii. 3–5.
3927 He could play the bagpipes . . . and mend nets.
3928 Turn wooden cups, and wrestle and shoot well (with a bow).
3929 He always carried a large knife at his belt.
3932 No one dared touch him; it was too dangerous.
3936 *market-betere*, a swaggering nuisance at markets.
3937–8 No one dared lay a finger on him without his swearing to make him
    pay for it directly.

That he ne swoor he sholde anon abegge.
A theef he was for sothe of corn and mele,   *in truth*
3940 And that a sly, and usaunt for to stele.   *accustomed*
His name was hoote deynous Symkyn.
A wyf he hadde, ycomen of noble kyn;   *family*
The person of the toun hir fader was.
With hire he yaf ful many a panne of bras,
3945 For that Symkyn sholde in his blood allye.
She was yfostred in a nonnerye;   *brought up*
For Symkyn wolde no wyf, as he sayde,
But she were wel ynorissed and a mayde,   *well bred*
To saven his estaat of yomanrye.
3950 And she was proud, and peert as is a pye.   *saucy; magpie*
A ful fair sighte was it upon hem two;
On halydayes biforn hire wolde he go   *religious festivals*
With his typet wound aboute his heed,   *tippet*
And she cam after in a gyte of reed;   *gown*
3955 And Symkyn hadde hosen of the same.
Ther dorste no wight clepen hire but 'dame';
Was noon so hardy that wente by the weye   *bold*
That with hire dorste rage or ones pleye,
But if he wolde be slayn of Symkyn   *unless*
3960 With panade, or with knyf, or boidekyn.   *dagger*
For jalous folk ben perilous everemo;   *dangerous*
Algate they wolde hire wyves wenden so.
And eek, for she was somdel smoterlich,
She was as digne as water in a dich,
3965 And ful of hoker and of bisemare.   *scorn; contempt*
Hir thoughte that a lady sholde hire spare,
What for hire kynrede and hir nortelrie
That she hadde lerned in the nonnerie.

3941 He was known as scornful Simkin (a diminutive of Simon).
3943 Her father was the village priest (i.e. she was illegitimate).
3944–5 He gave away with her a dowry of valuable brass pans, so that Simkin
    should marry into his family.
3949 To keep up his yeoman's rank.
3951 They made a handsome pair.
3956 No one dared call her anything but 'madam'. See *General Prologue* 376.
3958 Romp or even dally with her.
3962 At any rate they'd like their wives to think them so.
3963–4 Also, because she was somewhat sullied in reputation (by reason of her
    illegitimacy), she was as dignified as ditch-water (i.e. stinking with pride).
3966–7 It seemed to her that a lady should hold herself aloof, on account of her
    family background and her education.

A doghter hadde they bitwixe hem two   *between*
3970 Of twenty yeer, withouten any mo,   *other (children)*
Savynge a child that was of half yeer age;
In cradel it lay and was a propre page.   *fine-looking lad*
This wenche thikke and wel ygrowen was,   *plump*
With kamus nose, and eyen greye as glas,
3975 With buttokes brode, and brestes rounde and hye;
But right fair was hire heer, I wol nat lye.   *very pretty*
    This person of the toun, for she was feir,
In purpos was to maken hire his heir,
Bothe of his catel and his mesuage,   *goods; house*
3980 And straunge he made it of hir mariage.
His purpos was for to bistowe hire hye
Into som worthy blood of auncetrye;
For hooly chirches good moot been despended
On hooly chirches blood, that is descended.
3985 Therfore he wolde his hooly blood honoure,
Though that he hooly chirche sholde devoure.
    Greet sokene hath this millere, out of doute,   *toll*
With whete and malt of al the land aboute;
And nameliche ther was a greet collegge   *in particular*
3990 Men clepen the Soler Halle at Cantebregge;   *call*
Ther was hir whete and eek hir malt ygrounde.
And on a day it happed, in a stounde,   *happened suddenly*
Sik lay the maunciple on a maladye;
Men wenden wisly that he sholde dye.
3995 For which this millere stal bothe mele and corn   *stole*
An hundred tyme moore than biforn;
For therbiforn he stal but curteisly,   *politely*
But now he was a theef outrageously,
For which the wardeyn chidde and made fare.
4000 But therof sette the millere nat a tare;
He craketh boost, and swoor it was nat so.   *boasts loudly*
    Thanne were ther yonge povre scolers two,   *poor*
That dwelten in this halle, of which I seye.
Testif they were, and lusty for to pleye,
4005 And, oonly for hire myrthe and revelyre,
Upon the wardeyn bisily they crye   *eagerly; beg*

3977 *This person of the town*, the village priest (her grandfather).
3980 And he made difficulties about her marriage.
3983–4 For holy church's goods (i.e. the priest's *catel* and *mesuage*) must be
    spent on those descended from the blood of holy church (i.e. on his grand-
    daughter).
3986 Though he devoured holy church to do it.
3991 *Ther* i.e. at Simkin's mill.
3993 *maunciple*. See *General Prologue* 567.
3994 They were quite sure he was going to die.
3999 The warden (of the college) complained and made a to-do.
4000 But the miller didn't give a bean (lit. tare).
4004 They were headstrong and eager for a lark.

To yeve hem leve, but a litel stounde,   *while*
To goon to mille and seen hir corn ygrounde;
And hardily they dorste leye hir nekke
4010 The millere sholde not stele hem half a pekke
Of corn by sleighte, ne by force hem reve;   *trickery; rob*
And at the laste the wardeyn yaf hem leve.
John highte that oon, and Aleyn highte   *was called; Alan*
    that oother;
Of a toun were they born, that highte   *in the same village*
    Strother,
4015 Fer in the north, I kan nat telle where.
    This Aleyn maketh redy al his gere,
And on an hors the sak he caste anon.
Forth goth Aleyn the clerk, and also John,   *student*
With good swerd and with bokeler by hir syde.
4020 John knew the wey, – hem nedede no gyde, –   *they needed*
And at the mille the sak adoun he layth.
Aleyn spak first, 'Al hayl, Symond, y-fayth!   *welcome*
Hou fares thy faire doghter and thy wyf?'
    'Aleyn, welcome,' quod Symkyn, 'by my lyf!
4025 And John also, how now, what do ye heer?'
    'Symond,' quod John, 'by God, nede   *necessity*
      has na peer.   *equal*
Hym boes serve hymself that has na swayn,
Or elles he is a fool, as clerkes sayn.
Oure manciple, I hope he wil be deed,
4030 Swa werkes ay the wanges in his heed;
And forthy is I come, and eek Alayn,
To grynde oure corn and carie it ham agayn;   *home*
I pray yow spede us heythen that ye may.'
    'It shal be doon,' quod Symkyn, 'by my fay!   *faith*
4035 What wol ye doon whil that it is in hande?'
    'By God, right by the hopur wil I stande,'
Quod John, 'and se howgates the corn gas in.   *in what way*
Yet saugh I nevere, by my fader kyn,   *saw; father's*
How that the hopur wagges til and fra.'
4040   Aleyn answerde, 'John, and wiltow swa?   *so*
Thanne wil I be bynethe, by my croun,
And se how that the mele falles doun

4009 They were ready to wager their head.
4014–15 Chaucer mimics the Northern speech of the students in this tale, and
    does so with remarkable accuracy.
4027 A man who has no servant must serve himself.
4029–30 I expect he will die, his molar teeth are aching so much.
4031 And that's why I have come.
4033 Please help us to get away as quickly as you can.
4036 *hopur*, hopper, through which the grain passed into the mill.
4039 Waggles to and fro.
4041 *by my croun*, by my crown (an asseveration).

Into the trough; that sal be my disport.
For John, y-faith, I may been of youre sort;
4045 I is as ille a millere as ar ye.'   *poor*
        This millere smyled of hir nycetee,   *at; simplicity*
And thoghte, 'Al this nys doon but for a wyle.   *trick*
They wene that no man may hem bigyle,
But by my thrift, yet shal I blere hir ye,
4050 For al the sleighte in hir philosophye.   *cunning*
The moore queynte crekes that they make,   *artful tricks*
The moore wol I stele whan I take.
In stide of flour yet wol I yeve hem bren.   *instead; bran*
"The gretteste clerkes been noght wisest men,"
4055 As whilom to the wolf thus spak the mare.   *once*
Of al hir art ne counte I noght a tare.'
        Out at the dore he gooth ful pryvely,   *stealthily*
Whan that he saugh his tyme, softely.
He looketh up and doun til he hath founde
4060 The clerkes hors, ther as it stood ybounde
Bihynde the mille, under a levesel;   *leafy arbour*
And to the hors he goth hym faire and wel;
He strepeth of the brydel right anon.   *strips off*
And whan the hors was laus, he gynneth gon   *loose; raced*
4065 Toward the fen, ther wilde mares renne,
And forth with 'wehee,' thurgh thikke and thurgh
        thenne.   *thin*
        This millere gooth agayn, no word he seyde,
But dooth his note, and with the clerkes pleyde,   *job; joked*
Til that hir corn was faire and weel ygrounde.
4070 And whan the mele is sakked and ybounde,
This John goth out and fynt his hors away,
And gan to crie 'Harrow!' and 'Weylaway!
Oure hors is lorn, Alayn, for Goddes banes,   *lost; bones*
Step on thy feet! Com of, man, al atanes!
4075 Allas, our wardeyn has his palfrey lorn.'
This Aleyn al forgat, bothe mele and corn;
Al was out of his mynde his housbondrie.
'What, whilk way is he geen?' he gan to crie.   *which; gone*
        The wyf cam lepynge inward with a ren.
4080 She seyde, 'Allas! youre hors goth to the fen
With wilde mares, as faste as he may go.

4043 That'll be fun for me.
4044 I'm rather like you.
4049 But, as I live, I'll hoodwink them.
4055 An allusion to the Aesop fable of the Wolf and the Mare.
4062 And he goes up to the horse in a friendly manner.
4066 *wehee*, an imitation of the whinnying of a horse.
4072 *Harrow*, a cry for help; *Weylaway*, alas.
4074 Step lively! Come on, man, be quick!
4077 All thoughts of economy had fled from his mind.
4079 Came running in quickly.

Unthank come on his hand that boond hym so,
And he that bettre sholde han knyt the reyne!'   *fastened*
'Allas,' quod John, 'Aleyn, for Cristes peyne,
4085 Lay doun thy swerd, and I wil myn alswa.   *also*
I is ful wight, God waat, as is a raa;
By Goddes herte, he sal nat scape us bathe!   *escape; both*
Why ne had thow pit the capul in the lathe?
Ilhayl! by God, Alayn, thou is a fonne!'   *bad luck; fool*
4090   Thise sely clerkes han ful faste yronne   *wretched*
Toward the fen, bothe Aleyn and eek John.
And whan the millere saugh that they were gon,
He half a busshel of hir flour hath take,   *taken*
And bad his wyf go knede it in a cake.
4095 He seyde, 'I trowe the clerkes were aferd.
Yet kan a millere make a clerkes berd,
For al his art; now lat hem goon hir weye!
Lo, wher he gooth! ye, lat the children pleye.
They gete hym nat so lightly, by my croun.'   *easily*
4100   Thise sely clerkes rennen up and doun
With 'Keep! keep! stand! jossa, warderere,
Ga whistle thou, and I shal kepe hym heere!'   *go*
But shortly, til that it was verray nyght,   *briefly*
They koude nat, though they dide al hir myght,
4105 Hir capul cacche, he ran alwey so faste,   *always*
Til in a dych they caughte hym atte laste.
     Wery and weet, as beest is in the reyn,   *wet*
Comth sely John, and with him comth Aleyn.
'Allas,' quod John, 'the day that I was born!
4110 Now are we dryve til hethyng and til scorn.
Oure corn is stoln, men wil us fooles calle,
Bathe the wardeyn and oure felawes alle,   *friends*
And namely the millere, weylaway!'   *especially*
     Thus pleyneth John as he gooth by the way   *complains*
4115 Toward the mille, and Bayard in his hond.
The millere sittynge by the fyr he fond,   *found*
For it was nyght, and forther myghte they noght;
But for the love of God they hym bisoght
Of herberwe and of ese, as for hir peny.
4120   The millere seyde agayn, 'If ther be eny,

4082 Bad luck to the hand that tied him so carelessly.
4086 I'm as nimble, God knows, as a roe.
4088 Why didn't you put the nag in the barn?
4095 I think those students have had a fright.
4096 A miller can still deceive a student.
4101 Come up! stand! down here! look out behind!
4110 Now we're brought into contempt.
4115 Leading Bayard (a common name for a horse).
4117 And they could go no further.
4118–19 For the love of God, and for a penny, they begged him for shelter and hospitality.

Swich as it is, yet shal ye have youre part.   *such; share*
Myn hous is streit, but ye han lerned art;
Ye konne by argumentes make a place
A myle brood of twenty foot of space.   *broad; from*
4125 Lat se now if this place may suffise,   *let's see*
Or make it rowm with speche, as is youre gise.'
    'Now, Symond,' seyde John, 'by seint Cutberd,   *Cuthbert*
Ay is thou myrie, and this is faire answerd.
I have herd seyd, "man sal taa of twa thynges
4130 Slyk as he fyndes, or taa slyk as he brynges."
But specially I pray thee, hooste deere,
Get us som mete and drynke, and make us
    cheere,   *good cheer*
And we wil payen trewely atte fulle.   *in full*
With empty hand men may na haukes tulle;   *no; lure*
4135 Loo, heere oure silver, redy for to spende.'
    This millere into toun his doghter sende
For ale and breed, and rosted hem a goos,
And boond hire hors, it sholde namoore go loos;
And in his owene chambre hem made a bed,
4140 With sheetes and with chalons faire yspred,   *blankets*
Noght from his owene bed ten foot or twelve.
His doghter hadde a bed, al by hirselve,
Right in the same chambre by and by.
It myghte be no bet, and cause why?
4145 Ther was no roumer herberwe in the place.
They soupen and they speke, hem to   *to cheer themselves up*
    solace,
And drynken evere strong ale atte beste.
Aboute mydnyght wente they to reste.
    Wel hath this millere vernysshed his heed;   *oiled*
4150 Ful pale he was for dronken, and nat reed.
He yexeth, and he speketh thurgh the nose   *hiccoughs*
As he were on the quakke, or on the pose.
To bedde he goth, and with hym goth his wyf.
As any jay she light was and jolyf,   *spry; saucy*
4155 So was hir joly whistle wel ywet.
The cradel at hir beddes feet is set,

4122 My house is small, but you have studied the arts.
4126 Or talk it into being larger, in your usual fashion.
4128 You will have your little joke, and that's a fair answer.
4129–30 'A man must take one of two things – such as he finds or such as he
    brings,' i.e. a man must take things as he finds them.
4143 *by and by*, close by (her parents' bed).
4144 There was nothing else for it, and why?
4145 There was no larger room in the place.
4147 Drink strong ale with unflagging zeal.
4150 He looked quite pale with drink.
4152 As though he had asthma or a cold in the head.

To rokken, and to yeve the child to sowke.   *suck*
And whan that dronken al was in the crowke,   *jug*
To bedde wente the doghter right anon;
4160 To bedde goth Aleyn and also John;
Ther nas na moore, – hem nedede no dwale.
This millere hath so wisely bibbed ale
That as an hors he fnorteth in his sleep,   *snorts*
Ne of his tayl bihynde he took no keep.   *heed*
4165 His wyf bar hym a burdon, a ful strong;
Men myghte hir rowtyng heere two furlong;   *snoring*
The wenche rowteth eek, *par compaignye*.   *for company*
      Aleyn the clerk, that herde this melodye,
He poked John, and seyde, 'Slepestow?
4170 Herdestow evere slyk a sang er now?   *such; before*
Lo, swilk a complyn is ymel hem alle,
A wilde fyr upon thair bodyes falle!   *erysipelas*
Wha herkned evere slyk a ferly thyng?
Ye, they sal have the flour of il endyng.
4175 This lange nyght ther tydes me na reste;
But yet, nafors, al sal be for the beste.   *no matter*
For, John,' seyde he, 'als evere moot I thryve,
If that I may, yon wenche wil I swyve.   *copulate with*
Som esement has lawe yshapen us;
4180 For, John, ther is a lawe that says thus,
That gif a man in a point be agreved,
That in another he sal be releved.
Oure corn is stoln, sothly, it is na nay,
And we han had an il fit al this day;   *bad turn*
4185 And syn I sal have neen amendement   *no compensation*
Agayn my los, I will have esement.
By Goddes sale, it sal neen other bee!'
      This John answerde, 'Alayn, avyse thee!   *have a care*
The millere is a perilous man,' he seyde.
4190 'And gif that he out of his sleep abreyde,   *wakes up*
He myghte doon us bathe a vileynye.'   *great harm*
      Aleyn answerde, 'I counte hym nat a flye.'
And up he rist, and by the wenche he crepte.   *gets*
This wenche lay uprighte, and faste slepte,   *on her back*

4161 After that came silence – they needed no sleeping-draught.
4165 Accompanied him with a powerful bass. (See *General Prologue* 673.)
4171 They're singing compline (i.e. evening service) so well between them.
4173 Whoever heard such a weird noise?
4174 Yes, they'll have the worst of it in the end.
4175 I shan't sleep a wink the whole night.
4179 The law provides us some redress.
4183 It's true, there's no denying it.
4187 By God's soul, it shall not be otherwise!
4192 He's no more nuisance than a fly.

4195	Til he so ny was, er she myghte espie,	
	That it had been to late for to crie,	
	And shortly for to seyn, they were aton.	*united*
	Now pley, Aleyn, for I wol speke of John.	
	This John lith stille a furlong wey or two,	
4200	And to hymself he maketh routhe and wo.	
	'Allas!' quod he, 'this is a wikked jape;	*bad joke*
	Now may I seyn that I is but an ape.	
	Yet has my felawe somwhat for his harm;	
	He has the milleris doghter in his arm.	
4205	He auntred hym, and has his nedes sped,	
	And I lye as a draf-sak in my bed;	*sack of chaff*
	And when this jape is tald another day,	
	I sal been halde a daf, a cokenay!	
	I wil arise and auntre it, by my fayth!	
4210	"Unhardy is unseely," thus men sayth.'	
	And up he roos, and softely he wente	
	Unto the cradel, and in his hand it hente,	*took*
	And baar it softe unto his beddes feet.	
	Soone after this the wyf hir rowtyng leet,	*left off*
4215	And gan awake, and wente hire out to pisse,	*woke up*
	And cam agayn, and gan hir cradel mysse,	*missed*
	And groped heer and ther, but she foond noon.	
	'Allas!' quod she, 'I hadde almoost mysgoon;	
	I hadde almoost goon to the clerkes bed.	
4220	Ey, *benedicite!* thanne hadde I foule ysped.'	
	And forth she gooth til she the cradel fond.	
	She gropeth alwey forther with hir hond,	
	And foond the bed, and thoghte noght but good,	*all was well*
	By cause that the cradel by it stood,	
4225	And nyste wher she was, for it was derk;	*did not know*
	But faire and wel she creep in to the clerk,	*crept*
	And lith ful stille, and wolde han caught a sleep.	*gone to sleep*
	Withinne a while this John the clerk up leep,	*leapt*
	And on this goode wyf he leith on soore.	*lays on hard*
4230	So myrie a fit ne hadde she nat ful yoore;	
	He priketh harde and depe as he were mad.	
	This joly lyf han thise two clerkes lad	
	Til that the thridde cok bigan to synge.	

4195 He was so close to her before she noticed him.
4199 John lies still for a few minutes.
4200 He moans and grumbles to himself.
4205 He took a chance, and has done well for himself.
4208 I shall be held a sissy and a fool.
4210 'A coward has no luck.'
4213 Carried it gently to the foot of his bed.
4218 I nearly went astray.
4220 Eh, bless us, then I'd have had a bad time of it.
4230 She hadn't had such a merry bout for ages.
4233 *thridde cok*, i.e. near dawn.

Aleyn wax wery in the dawenynge,
4235 For he had swonken al the longe nyght,   *toiled*
And seyde, 'Fare weel, Malyne, sweete   *Molly*
    wight!   *creature*
The day is come, I may no lenger byde;
But everemo, wher so I go or ryde,
I is thyn awen clerk, swa have I seel!'
4240   'Now deere lemman,' quod she, 'go, far weel!   *sweetheart*
But er thow go, o thyng I wol thee telle:
Whan that thou wendest homward by the melle,   *mill*
Right at the entree of the dore bihynde
Thou shalt a cake of half a busshel fynde   *loaf*
4245 That was ymaked of thyn owene mele,
Which that I heelp my sire for to stele.   *helped; father*
And, goode lemman, God thee save and kepe!'
And with that word almoost she gan to wepe.
    Aleyn up rist, and thoughte, 'Er that it dawe,   *dawns*
4250 I wol go crepen in by my felawe';
And fond the cradel with his hand anon.
'By God,' thoughte he, 'al wrang I have mysgon.
Myn heed is toty of my swynk to-nyght,
That makes me that I ga nat aright.
4255 I woot wel by the cradel I have mysgo;
Heere lith the millere and his wyf also.'
And forth he goth, a twenty devel way,
Unto the bed ther as the millere lay.
He wende have cropen by his felawe John,
4260 And by the millere in he creep anon,
And caughte hym by the nekke, and softe he
    spak.
He seyde, 'Thou John, thou swynes-heed, awak,   *hogshead*
For Cristes saule, and heer a noble game.   *hear*
For by that lord that called is seint Jame,
4265 As I have thries in this shorte nyght
Swyved the milleres doghter bolt upright,   *flat on her back*
Whil thow hast, as a coward, been agast.'   *scared*
    'Ye, false harlot,' quod the millere, 'hast?   *rogue*
A, false traitour! false clerk!' quod he,
4270 'Thow shalt be deed, by Goddes dignitee!   *die*
Who dorste be so boold to disparage
My doghter, that is come of swich lynage?'

4238 Evermore, wherever I walk or ride (i.e. through thick and thin).
4239 I am your own true student, as I hope for happiness.
4243 Just near the back door.
4253 My head is dizzy with my toil this night.
4254 That's why I'm not going the right way.
4257 *a twenty devel way*, i.e. with devilish bad luck.
4259 He thought he was creeping in with his companion John.
4271 How dare you be so bold as to dishonour.

And by the throte-bolle he caughte Alayn,   *Adam's apple*
And he hente hym despitously agayn,
4275 And on the nose he smoot hym with his fest.   *fist*
Doun ran the blody streem upon his brest;
And in the floor, with nose and mouth tobroke,   *broken*
They walwe as doon two pigges in a poke;   *roll about; bag*
And up they goon, and doun agayn anon,
4280 Til that the millere sporned at a stoon,   *tripped over*
And doun he fil bakward upon his wyf,
That wiste no thyng of this nyce stryf;   *knew; foolish*
For she was falle aslepe a lite wight
With John the clerk, that waked hadde al nyght,
4285 And with the fal out of hir sleep she breyde.   *started*
'Help! hooly croys of Bromeholm,' she seyde,
'*In manus tuas!* Lord, to thee I calle!
Awak, Symond! the feend is on me falle.   *fallen*
Myn herte is broken; help! I nam but deed!
4290 Ther lyth oon upon my wombe and on myn heed.   *someone*
Help, Symkyn, for the false clerkes fighte!'
    This John stirte up as faste as ever he myghte,
And graspeth by the walles to and fro,   *gropes*
To fynde a staf; and she stirte up also,
4295 And knew the estres bet than did this John,   *interior*
And by the wal a staf she foond anon,
And saugh a litel shymeryng of a light,   *glimmer*
For at an hole in shoon the moone bright;
And by that light she saugh hem bothe two,
4300 But sikerly she nyste who was who,   *certainly*
But as she saugh a whit thyng in hir ye.
And whan she gan this white thyng espye,
She wende the clerk hadde wered a volupeer,
And with the staf she drow ay neer and neer,   *drew; nearer*
4305 And wende han hit this Aleyn at the fulle,
And smoot the millere on the pyled skulle,   *bald*
That doun he gooth, and cride, 'Harrow! I dye!'   *so that*
Thise clerkes beete hym weel and lete hym lye;
And greythen hem, and tooke hir hors anon,   *get ready*
4310 And eek hire mele, and on hir wey they gon.
And at the mille yet they tooke hir cake
Of half a busshel flour, ful wel ybake.   *baked*

4274 And he (Alan) furiously grabbed back at him.
4283 For she had just fallen asleep.
4287 *In manus tuas*, into thy hands (I commend my spirit): Luke xxiii, 46.
4289 I'm as good as dead.
4301 Except that she saw a white thing.
4303 She thought the student had been wearing a nightcap.
4305 With the idea of hitting Alan a great wallop.

Thus is the proude millere wel ybete,	*beaten*
And hath ylost the gryndynge of the whete,	
4315 And payed for the soper everideel	
Of Aleyn and of John, that bette hym weel.	*beat*
His wyf is swyved, and his doghter als.	*also*
Lo, swich it is a millere to be fals!	
And therfore this proverbe is seyd ful sooth,	*truly*
4320 'Hym thar nat wene wel that yvele dooth';	
A gylour shal hymself bigyled be.	*trickster*
And God, that sitteth heighe in magestee,	
Save al this compaignye, grete and smale!	
Thus have I quyt the Millere in my tale.	*paid back*

Heere is ended the Reves Tale

4314 *ylost*, got no payment for.
4315 Paid in full for the supper.
4318 See what comes of being a dishonest miller.
4320 'He must not expect good who does evil.'

The Cook's Prologue

The Prologe of the Cokes Tale

4325 THE COOK of Londoun, whil the Reve spak,
For joye him thoughte he clawed him on the bak.
'Ha! ha!' quod he, 'for Cristes passion,
This millere hadde a sharp conclusion
Upon his argument of herbergage!
4330 Wel seyde Salomon in his langage,
"Ne bryng nat every man into thyn hous";
For herberwynge by nyghte is perilous.
Wel oghte a man avysed for to be
Whom that he broghte into his pryvetee.
4335 I pray to God, so yeve me sorwe and care   *give*
If evere, sitthe I highte Hogge of Ware,
Herde I a millere bettre yset a-werk.
He hadde a jape of malice in the derk.
But God forbede that we stynte heere;   *stop*
4340 And therfore, if ye vouche-sauf to heere
A tale of me, that am a povre man,   *poor*
I wol you telle, as wel as evere I kan,
A litel jape that fil in oure citee.'   *joke; happened*
    Oure Hoost answerde and seide, 'I graunte it thee.
4345 Now telle on, Roger, looke that it be good;
For many a pastee hastow laten blood,
And many a Jakke of Dovere hastow soold
That hath been twies hoot and twies coold.
Of many a pilgrym hastow Cristes curs,
4350 For of thy percely yet they fare the wors,
That they han eten with thy stubbel goos;
For in thy shoppe is many a flye loos.   *loose*

4326 In his joy it seemed to him that the Reeve was scratching his back, i.e. he had the sort of pleasure he would have felt if the Reeve had been scratching an itch on his back.
4329 To his argument about a lodging for the night. (See *Reeve's Tale* 4122 ff.)
4331 Ecclus. xi. 29.
4333–4 A man certainly ought to be careful about whom he welcomes into the privacy of his own home.
4336 Since I was called Hodge of Ware.
4337 I heard of a miller scored off more neatly.
4338 He had a spiteful trick played on him in the dark.
4346 Many a pasty have you let blood, i.e. drained of its gravy.
4347 *Jakke of Dovere*, a warmed-up pie.
4350 For they're still feeling the effects of that parsley of yours.
4351 *stubbel goos*, an old goose fed on stubble.

Now telle on, gentil Roger by thy name.   *worthy*
But yet I pray thee, be nat wroth for game;
4355   A man may seye ful soothe in game and pley.'
    'Thou seist ful sooth,' quod Roger, 'by my fey!
But "sooth pley, quaad pley," as the Flemyng seith.
And therfore, Herry Bailly, by thy feith,   *Harry*
Be thou nat wrooth, er we departen heer,
4360   Though that my tale be of an hostileer.   *innkeeper*
But nathelees I wol nat telle it yit;
But er we parte, ywis, thou shalt be quit.'   *certainly; paid back*
And therwithal he lough and made cheere,
And seyde his tale, as ye shul after heere.

The Cook's Tale

Heere bigynneth the Cookes Tale

4365   A PRENTYS whilom dwelled in oure citee,   *apprentice; once*
And of a craft of vitailliers was hee.   *victuallers*
Gaillard he was as goldfynch in the shawe,   *gay; wood*
Broun as a berye, a propre short felawe,
With lokkes blake, ykembd ful fetisly.   *combed; neatly*
4370   Dauncen he koude so wel and jolily   *merrily*
That he was cleped Perkyn Revelour.   *called; the Reveller*
He was as ful of love and paramour   *love-making*
As is the hyve ful of hony sweete:
Wel was the wenche with hym myghte meete.
4375   At every bridale wolde he synge and hoppe;
He loved bet the taverne than the shoppe.   *better*
For whan ther any ridyng was in Chepe,

4354   Don't be angry at a little fun.
4355   i.e. there's many a true word spoken in jest.
4356   You're quite right . . . upon my word.
4357   'A true jest is a bad jest.'
4363   And with that he laughed and made merry.
4368   A short, good-looking fellow.
4374   Happy the wench that chanced to meet him.
4377   Any procession in Cheapside.

Out of the shoppe thider wolde he lepe –
Til that he hadde al the sighte yseyn,   *seen*
4380 And daunced wel, he wolde nat come ayeyn –   *back*
And gadered hym a meynee of his sort
To hoppe and synge and maken swich disport;
And ther they setten stevene for to meete,
To pleyen at the dys in swich a streete.   *such and such*
4385 For in the toune nas ther no prentys   *was not*
That fairer koude caste a paire of dys   *better*
Than Perkyn koude, and therto he was free   *besides*
Of his dispense, in place of pryvetee.
That fond his maister wel in his chaffare;
4390 For often tyme he foond his box ful bare.
For sikerly a prentys revelour   *certainly*
That haunteth dys, riot, or paramour,
His maister shal it in his shoppe abye,   *pay dearly for*
Al have he no part of the mynstralcye.
4395 For thefte and riot, they been convertible
Al konne he pleye on gyterne or ribible.
Revel and trouthe, as in a lowe degree,
They been ful wrothe al day, as men may see.
This joly prentys with his maister bood,   *stayed*
4400 Til he were ny out of his prentishood,   *nearly*
Al were he snybbed bothe erly and late,
And somtyme lad with revel to Newegate.
But atte laste his maister hym bithoghte,
Upon a day, whan he his papir soughte,

4378 He would dash towards it.
4381–2 Gathered round him a crowd of people of his own sort to dance, sing,
   and have fun.
4383 They made a date to meet.
4388 In his spending, on the quiet.
4389 His master found good evidence of this in his daily business.
4392 Who makes a practice of dicing, wenching, and riotous living.
4394–6 Although he (the master) has no share in the musical entertainment,
   and his apprentice enjoys himself playing on a guitar or fiddle; for theft and
   riotous living are interchangeable. (The meaning is that the master pays the
   piper, while his dishonest servant calls the tune.)
4397–8 Revelry and honesty, in a man of low degree, are always at odds with
   each other.
4401 Although he was continually being reprimanded.
4402 Sometimes led off with minstrelsy to jail. (In Chaucer's day disorderly
   persons were marched off to prison to the sound of music, which was meant to
   advertise their disgrace.)
4403–4 At last his master called to mind, when he was examining his accounts
   one day.

4405	Of a proverbe that seith this same word,	
	'Wel bet is roten appul out of hoord	
	Than that it rotie al the remenaunt.'	
	So fareth it by a riotous servaunt;	
	It is ful lasse harm to lete hym pace,	*much less; go*
4410	Than he shende alle the servantz in the place.	*ruin*
	Therfore his maister yaf hym acquitance,	*release*
	And bad hym go, with sorwe and with meschance!	
	And thus this joly prentys hadde his leve.	
	Now lat hym riote al the nyghte or leve.	
4415	And for ther is no theef withoute a lowke,	*since; accomplice*
	That helpeth hym to wasten and to sowke	*embezzle*
	Of that he brybe kan or borwe may,	*steal*
	Anon he sente his bed and his array	*clothing*
	Unto a compeer of his owene sort,	*comrade*
4420	That lovede dys, and revel, and disport,	*pleasure*
	And hadde a wyf that heeld for contenance	
	A shoppe, and swyved for hir sustenance.	*copulated; living*

*   *   *   *

4406–7 'Better remove a rotten apple from the store than let it rot the rest.'
4408 So it is with a dissolute servant.
4412 *with sorwe and with meschance*, and bad luck go with him.
4414 Now let him revel or not all night, as he likes.
4421–2 Who kept a shop for the sake of appearances.

The Shipman's Tale

Heere bigynneth the Shipmannes Tale

A MARCHANT whilom dwelled at Seint-Denys,	*once*
That riche was, for which men helde hym wys,	*prudent*
A wyf he hadde of excellent beautee;	
And compaignable and revelous was she,	
5 Which is a thyng that causeth more dispence	*expense*
Than worth is al the chiere and reverence	
That men hem doon at festes and at daunces.	*feasts*
Swiche salutaciouns and contenaunces	*pretences*
Passen as dooth a shadwe upon the wal;	
10 But wo is hym that payen moot for al!	*must*
The sely housbonde, algate he moot paye,	
He moot us clothe, and he moot us arraye,	
Al for his owene worshipe richely,	
In which array we daunce jolily.	*merrily*
15 And if that he noght may, par aventure,	*perhaps*
Or ellis list no swich dispence endure,	
But thynketh it is wasted and ylost,	
Thanne moot another payen for oure cost,	
Or lene us gold, and that is perilous.	*lend*
20 This noble marchaunt heeld a worthy hous,	
For which he hadde alday so greet repair	
For his largesse, and for his wyf was fair,	*liberality*
That wonder is; but herkneth to my tale.	
Amonges alle his gestes, grete and smale,	
25 Ther was a monk, a fair man and a boold –	
I trowe a thritty wynter he was oold –	
That evere in oon was drawynge to that place.	
This yonge monk, that was so fair of face,	

4 She was sociable and fond of revelry.
6 Than all the greetings and compliments are worth.
11 The wretched husband always foots the bill.
12–13 He must dress us handsomely if only to do himself credit. (*us* apparently means 'us women'; it therefore looks as if this tale was originally meant for a woman, probably the Wife of Bath.)
16 Or else will not put up with such expense.
21 And so he was always having visitors.
26 I should think he was some thirty years old.
27 Who was continually visiting that place.

Aqueynted was so with the goode man,
30 Sith that hir firste knoweliche bigan,
That in his hous as famulier was he   *at home*
As it is possible any freend to be.
    And for as muchel as this goode man,   *much*
And eek this monk, of which that I bigan,
35 Were bothe two yborn in o village,
The monk hym claymeth as for cosynage;
And he agayn, he seith nat ones nay,
But was as glad therof as fowel of day;
For to his herte it was a greet plesaunce.   *pleasure*
40 Thus been they knyt with eterne alliaunce,   *joined; eternal*
And ech of hem gan oother for t'assure
Of bretherhede, whil that hir lyf may dure.
    Free was daun John, and manly of dispence,
As in that hous, and ful of diligence
45 To doon plesaunce, and also greet costage.
He noght forgat to yeve the leeste page
In al that hous; but after hir degree,   *according to their rank*
He yaf the lord, and sitthe al his meynee,   *then; household*
Whan that he cam, som manere honest thyng;
50 For which they were as glad of his comyng
As fowel is fayn whan that the sonne up riseth.   *glad*
Na moore of this as now, for it suffiseth.
    But so bifel, this marchant on a day
Shoop hym to make redy his array
55 Toward the toun of Brugges for to fare,   *Bruges; go*
To byen there a porcioun of ware;
For which he hath to Parys sent anon
A messenger, and preyed hath daun John   *messenger*
That he sholde come to Seint-Denys to pleye   *take a holiday*
60 With hym and with his wyf a day or tweye,
Er he to Brugges wente, in alle wise.
    This noble monk, of which I yow devyse,   *tell*
Hath of his abbot, as hym list, licence,

29–30 Had become so friendly with the good man since their first acquaintance.
35 Both born in the same village.
36 Claims kinship with him.
37–8 And he (the merchant) did not once deny it, but welcomed it as gladly as
     a bird the dawn.
41–2 They swore brotherhood with each other.
43 Sir John was open-handed, and generous in spending.
45 And also to go to great expense.
46 He did not forget to give something to the humblest page.
49 Some decent sort of present.
54 Set about making preparations.
56 To buy there a certain quantity of merchandise.
57 And so he immediately sent to Paris.
63 Has permission from his abbot, whenever he pleases.

By cause he was a man of heigh prudence,
65 And eek an officer, out for to ryde,
To seen hir graunges and hire bernes wyde,
And unto Seint-Denys he comth anon.
Who was so welcome as my lord daun John,
Oure deere cosyn, ful of curteisye?
70 With hym broghte he a jubbe of malvesye,   *jug; malmsey*
And eek another, ful of fyn vernage,
And volatyl, as ay was his usage,
And thus I lete hem ete and drynke and pleye,   *leave*
This marchant and this monk, a day or tweye.

75   The thridde day, this marchant up ariseth,
And on his nedes sadly hym avyseth,
And up into his countour-hous gooth he   *counting-house*
To rekene with hymself, wel may be,
Of thilke yeer how that it with hym stood,
80 And how that he despended hadde his good,   *spent; money*
And if that he encressed were or noon.   *richer; not*
His bookes and his bagges many oon   *a one*
He leith biforn hym on his countyng-   *counting-house table*
     bord.
Ful riche was his tresor and his hord,   *hoarded wealth*
85 For which ful faste his countour-dore he shette;
And eek he nolde that no man sholde hym lette
Of his acountes, for the meene tyme;
And thus he sit til it was passed pryme.   *sits; 9 a.m.*
Daun John was rysen in the morwe also,   *early morning*
90 And in the gardyn walketh to and fro,
And hath his thynges seyd ful curteisly.
     This goode wyf cam walkynge pryvely   *stealthily*
Into the gardyn, there he walketh softe,   *softly*
And hym saleweth, as she hath doon ofte.   *greets*
95 A mayde child cam in hire compaignye,
Which as hir list she may governe and gye,
For yet under the yerde was the mayde.
'O deere cosyn myn, daun John,' she sayde,

---

65 *out for to ryde.* See *General Prologue* 166.
66 To supervise their granges and their spacious barns.
71 *vernage*, an Italian wine.
72 And wild-fowl, as he always did.
76 And gives serious thought to his affairs.
78–9 To reckon up by himself, as near as he could, how things stood with him
     that year.
85 And so he shut fast his counting-house door.
86–7 He wanted no one to disturb him at his reckoning in the mean time.
91 Reverently said the things he had to say, i.e. the divine office in the breviary.
96–7 Whom she can instruct and govern as she likes, for the maiden was still
     under her authority.

'What eyleth yow so rathe for to ryse?'
100   'Nece,' quod he, 'it oghte ynough   *ought to be enough*
     suffise
Fyve houres for to slepe upon a nyght,
But it were for an old appalled wight,
As been thise wedded men, that lye and dare   *cower*
As in a fourme sit a wery hare,
105   Were al forstraught with houndes grete and smale.
But deere nece, why be ye so pale?
I trowe, certes, that oure goode man
Hath yow laboured sith the nyght bigan,
That yow were nede to resten hastily.'
110   And with that word he lough ful murily,   *laughed*
And of his owene thought he wax al reed.
    This faire wyf gan for to shake hir heed
And seyde thus, 'Ye, God woot al,' quod she.
'Nay, cosyn myn, it stant nat so with me;   *stands*
115   For, by that God that yaf me soule and lyf,   *gave*
In al the reawme of France is ther no wyf   *realm*
That lasse lust hath to that sory pley.
For I may synge "allas and weylawey,
That I was born," but to no wight,' quod she,   *no one*
120   'Dar I nat telle how that it stant with me.
Wherfore I thynke out of this land to wende,   *go*
Or elles of myself to make an ende,
So ful am I of drede and eek of care.'   *fear; sorrow*
    This monk bigan upon this wyf to stare,
125   And seyde, 'Allas, my nece, God forbede
That ye, for any sorwe or any drede,
Fordo youreself; but telleth me youre grief.   *destroy*
Paraventure I may, in youre meschief,   *perhaps; misfortune*
Conseille or helpe; and therfore telleth me
130   Al youre anoy, for it shal been secree.   *trouble; secret*
For on my porthors I make an ooth   *breviary*
That nevere in my lyf, for lief ne looth,   *friend or foe*
Ne shal I of no conseil yow biwreye.'
    'The same agayn to yow,' quod she, 'I seye.
135   By God and by this porthors I yow swere,
Though men me wolde al into pieces tere,   *tear*

99   What's wrong with you that you are up so early?
102   Except for a decrepit old creature.
104   Like a weary hare in its form.
105   Which is distracted by hounds.
109   So that you have urgent need to rest.
111   And blushed a bright red at his own thoughts.
113   God knows all, i.e. God knows it is not what you imagine.
117   Who takes less pleasure in that wretched sport.
133   Shall I betray any secret of yours.

Ne shal I nevere, for to goon to helle,
Biwreye a word of thyng that ye me telle,   *anything*
Nat for no cosynage ne alliance,
140 But verraily, for love and affiance.'   *trust*
Thus been they sworn, and heerupon they kiste,
And ech of hem tolde oother what hem liste.   *they pleased*
'Cosyn,' quod she, 'if that I hadde a space,   *opportunity*
As I have noon, and namely in this place,   *none; especially*
145 Thanne wolde I telle a legende of my lyf,   *story*
What I have suffred sith I was a wyf   *since*
With myn housbonde, al be he youre cosyn.'   *although he is*
'Nay,' quod this monk, 'by God and seint Martyn,
He is na moore cosyn unto me
150 Than is this leef that hangeth on the tree!
I clepe hym so, by Seint Denys of Fraunce,   *call*
To have the moore cause of aqueyntaunce
Of yow, which I have loved specially
Aboven alle wommen, sikerly.   *truly*
155 This swere I yow on my professioun.
Telleth youre grief, lest that he come adoun;   *down*
And hasteth yow, and gooth youre wey anon.'   *be quick*
'My deere love,' quod she, 'O my daun John,
Ful lief were me this conseil for to hyde,
160 But out it moot, I may namoore abyde.   *must; bear it*
Myn housbonde is to me the worste man
That evere was sith that the world bigan.
But sith I am a wyf, it sit nat me
To tellen no wight of oure privetee,   *anyone; private affairs*
165 Neither abedde, ne in noon oother place;
God shilde I sholde it tellen, for his grace!
A wyf ne shal nat seyn of hir housbonde
But al honour, as I kan understonde;
Save unto yow thus muche I tellen shal: *except*
170 As helpe me God, he is noght worth at al   *so*
In no degree the value of a flye.
But yet me greveth moost his nygardye.   *miserliness*
And wel ye woot that wommen naturelly
Desiren thynges sixe as wel as I: *six*
175 They wolde that hir housbondes sholde be
Hardy, and wise, and riche, and therto free,   *brave; generous*
And buxom unto his wyf, and fressh abedde.   *obedient; lively*
But by that ilke Lord that for us bledde,

---

137 Though I went to hell for it.
139 And this I do, not for kinship.
152–3 To have a better excuse for knowing you.
159 I'd dearly like to keep this secret hidden.
163 It's unbecoming of me.
166 God forbid I should tell it, by His grace!
168 Anything but what is honourable.

For his honour, myself for to arraye,
180 A Sonday next I moste nedes paye   *on*
An hundred frankes, or ellis I am lorn.   *ruined*
Yet were me levere that I were unborn
Than me were doon a sclaundre or vileynye;
And if myn housbonde eek it myghte espye,
185 I nere but lost; and therfore I yow preye,
Lene me this somme, or ellis moot I deye.   *lend; must*
Daun John, I seye, lene me thise hundred frankes.
Pardee, I wol nat faille yow my thankes,
If that yow list to doon that I yow praye.
190 For at a certeyn day I wol yow paye,
And doon to yow what plesance and service   *pleasure*
That I may doon, right as yow list devise.
And but I do, God take on me vengeance,   *unless*
As foul as evere hadde Genylon of France.'
195   This gentil monk answerde in this manere: *noble*
'Now trewely, myn owene lady deere,
I have,' quod he, 'on yow so greet a routhe   *pity*
That I yow swere, and plighte yow my trouthe,   *troth*
That whan youre housbonde is to Flaundres fare,   *gone*
200 I wol delyvere yow out of this care;   *anxiety*
For I wol brynge yow an hundred frankes.'
And with that word he caughte hire by the flankes,
And hire embraceth harde, and kiste hire ofte.
'Gooth now youre wey,' quod he, 'al stille and softe,   *quietly*
205 And lat us dyne as soone as that ye may;
For by my chilyndre it is pryme of day.
Gooth now, and beeth as trewe as I shal be.'
    'Now elles God forbede, sire,' quod she;
And forth she gooth as jolif as a pye,   *merry; magpie*
210 And bad the cookes that they sholde hem hye,   *hurry*
So that men myghte dyne, and that anon.
Up to hir housbonde is this wyf ygon,
And knokketh at his countour boldely.
    '*Quy la?*' quod he. 'Peter! it am I,'   *who's there?*
215 Quod she, 'what, sire, how longe wol ye faste?
How longe tyme wol ye rekene and caste
Youre sommes, and youre bookes, and youre thynges?

179 In order to dress myself in a way that will do him credit.
182–3 I'd rather never have been born than expose myself to slander or
    reproach.
184–5 If my husband were to find out, I'd be as good as lost.
188–9 Indeed, I shan't fail to thank you, if you are willing to do what I ask.
192 Just as you care to suggest.
194 *Genylon.* See *Nun's Priest's Tale* 4024.
206 For by my cylinder (i.e. portable sun-dial) it is 9 a.m.

The devel have part on alle swiche rekenynges!

Ye have ynough, pardee, of Goddes sonde;   *gifts*

220 Com doun to-day, and lat youre bagges stonde.

Ne be ye nat ashamed that daun John

Shal fasting al this day alenge goon?   *miserable*

What! lat us heere a messe, and go we dyne.'   *mass*

'Wyf,' quod this man, 'litel kanstow devyne   *guess*

225 The curious bisynesse that we have.   *complicated*

For of us chapmen, also God me save,   *merchants*

And by that lord that clepid is Seint Yve,   *called*

Scarsly amonges twelve tweye shul thryve

Continuelly, lastynge unto oure age.

230 We may wel make chiere and good visage,

And dryve forth the world as it may be,

And kepen oure estaat in pryvetee,

Til we be deed, or elles that we pleye

A pilgrymage, or goon out of the weye.

235 And therfore have I greet necessitee

Upon this queynte world t'avyse me;

For everemoore we moote stonde in drede   *fear*

Of hap and fortune in oure chapmanhede.   *chance; trading*

To Flaundres wol I go to-morwe at day,   *daybreak*

240 And come agayn, as soone as evere I may.

For which, my deere wyf, I thee biseke,

As be to every wight buxom and meke,   *everyone; obedient*

And for to keep oure good be curious,

And honestly governe wel oure hous.   *honourably*

245 Thou hast ynough, in every maner wise,   *way*

That to a thrifty houshold may suffise.

Thee lakketh noon array ne no vitaille;   *clothes; food*

Of silver in thy purs shaltow nat faille.'

And with that word his countour-dore he shette,   *shut*

250 And doun he gooth, no lenger wolde he lette.   *delay*

But hastily a messe was ther seyd,

And spedily the tables were yleyd,   *laid*

And to the dyner faste they hem spedde,   *hurried*

And richely this monk the chapman fedde.

255   At after-dyner daun John sobrely

This chapman took apart, and prively

218 May the devil have a share in all such reckonings.

228–9 Hardly two in twelve will stay prosperous till old age.

230–4 Well may we try to be cheerful and put a good face on things, and make what show we can in the world, and keep our affairs secret till we die; or, failing all this, try to find relaxation on a pilgrimage, or go somewhere out of the way (of creditors).

236 To consider this curious world with care.

243 And be careful to look after our goods.

254 The merchant fed the monk with sumptuous fare.

255–6 During the interval after dinner Sir John gravely took the merchant aside.

He seyde hym thus: 'Cosyn, it standeth so,
That wel I se to Brugges wol ye go.
God and seint Austyn spede yow and gyde!   *prosper*
260 I prey yow, cosyn, wisely that ye ryde.   *prudently*
Governeth yow also of youre diete
Atemprely, and namely in this hete.
Bitwix us two nedeth no strange fare;
Farewel, cosyn; God shilde yow fro care!   *shield*
265 And if that any thyng by day or nyght,
If it lye in my power and my myghte,
That ye me wol comande in any wyse,
It shal be doon, right as ye wol devyse.   *exactly; say*
     O thyng, er that ye goon, if it may be,
270 I wolde prey yow; for to lene me   *lend*
An hundred frankes, for a wyke or tweye,   *week*
For certein beestes that I moste beye,   *must buy*
To stoore with a place that is oures.
God helpe me so, I wolde it were youres!
275 I shal nat faille surely of my day,
Nat for a thousand frankes, a mile way.
But lat this thyng be secree, I yow preye,   *secret*
For yet to-nyght thise beestes moot I beye.
And fare now wel, myn owene cosyn deere;
280 Graunt mercy of youre cost and of youre cheere.'
     This noble marchant gentilly anon   *kindly*
Answerde and seyde, 'O cosyn myn, daun John,
Now sikerly this is a smal requeste.   *certainly*
My gold is youres, whan that it yow leste,   *you like*
285 And nat oonly my gold, but my chaffare.   *wares*
Take, what yow list, God shilde that ye spare.
     But o thyng is, ye knowe it wel ynogh,
Of chapmen, that hir moneie is hir plogh.   *money; plough*
We may creaunce whil we have a name;
290 But goldlees for to be, it is no game.
Paye it agayn whan it lith in youre ese;
After my myght ful fayn wolde I yow plese.'
     Thise hundred frankes he fette forth anon,   *fetched out*
And prively he took hem to daun John.   *secretly; gave*

261–2 Be moderate in your diet, especially in this heat.
263 Between us two there's no need for reserve.
273 To stock up a place of ours.
275 I will not fail to keep my day (for payment).
276 By as much as twenty minutes (i.e. the average time for walking a mile).
280 Many thanks for your generosity and hospitality.
286 God forbid you should be sparing.
289 We can get credit while our name is good.
291 When it's convenient to you.
292 I'm very glad to do what I can to please you.

295	No wight in al this world wiste of this loone,	*knew; loan*
	Savynge this marchant and daun John allone.	
	They drynke, and speke, and rome a while and pleye,	*loiter*
	Til that daun John rideth to his abbeye.	
	The morwe cam, and forth this marchant rideth	
300	To Flaundres-ward; his prentys wel hym gydeth,	
	Til he cam into Brugges murily.	*happily*
	Now gooth this marchant faste and bisily	
	Aboute his nede, and byeth and	*business*
	creaunceth.	*obtains credit*
	He neither pleyeth at the dees ne daunceth,	*dice*
305	But as a marchaunt, shortly for to telle,	*briefly*
	He let his lyf, and there I lete hym dwelle.	*leads; leave*
	The Sonday next the marchant was agon,	
	To Seint-Denys ycomen is daun John,	
	With crowne and berd al fressh and newe yshave.	*shaven*
310	In al the hous ther nas so litel a knave,	
	Ne no wight elles, that he nas ful fayn	
	That my lord daun John was come agayn.	
	And shortly to the point right for to gon	
	This faire wyf acorded with daun John	*agreed*
315	That for thise hundred frankes he sholde al nyght	
	Have hire in his armes bolt upright;	*flat on her back*
	And this acord parfourned was in dede.	
	In myrthe al nyght a bisy lyf they lede	
	Til it was day, that daun John wente his way,	*when*
320	And bad the meynee 'farewel, have good day!'	*household*
	For noon of hem, ne no wight in the toun,	
	Hath of daun John right no suspecioun.	
	And forth he rydeth hoom to his abbeye,	
	Or where hym list; namoore of hym I seye.	*he pleases*
325	This marchant, whan that ended was the faire,	
	To Seint-Denys he gan for to repaire,	*went home*
	And with his wyf he maketh feeste and cheere,	
	And telleth hire that chaffare is so deere	*merchandise*
	That nedes moste he make a chevyssaunce;	
330	For he was bounden in a reconyssaunce	
	To paye twenty thousand sheeld anon.	*crowns*
	For which this marchant is to Parys gon	

300 Towards Flanders; his apprentice guides him well.
307 The very next Sunday after the merchant had gone.
310–11 There was no serving-lad, however small, nor anyone else, who was
not very glad.
317 This agreement was carried out to the letter.
322 Has the least suspicion of Sir John.
327 He feasts and makes merry.
329 That he would have to raise a loan.
330 For he was bound by a recognizance.

To borwe of certeine freendes that he hadde   *from*
A certeyn frankes; and somme with him he ladde.
335 And whan that he was come into the toun,
For greet chiertee and greet affeccioun,   *fondness*
Unto daun John he first gooth hym to   *to enjoy himself*
     pleye;
Nat for to axe or borwe of hym moneye,   *ask*
But for to wite and seen of his welfare,
340 And for to tellen hym of his chaffare,   *trading*
As freendes doon whan they been met yfeere.   *together*
Daun John hym maketh feeste and murye cheere,
And he hym tolde agayn, ful specially,
How he hadde wel yboght and graciously,   *favourably*
345 Thanked be God, al hool his marchandise;
Save that he moste, in alle maner wise,   *by all means*
Maken a chevyssaunce, as for his beste,
And thanne he sholde been in joye and reste.   *peace of mind*
     Daun John answerde, 'Certes, I am fayn   *glad*
350 That ye in heele ar comen hom agayn.   *safe and sound*
And if that I were riche, as have I blisse,
Of twenty thousand sheeld sholde ye nat mysse,   *crowns; lack*
For ye so kyndely this oother day
Lente me gold; and as I kan and may,
355 I thanke yow, by God and by seint Jame!   *James*
But nathelees, I took unto oure dame,   *gave; lady*
Youre wyf, at hom, the same gold ageyn   *home*
Upon youre bench; she woot it wel, certeyn,
By certeyn tokenes that I kan hire telle.
360 Now, by youre leve, I may no lenger dwelle;
Oure abbot wole out of this toun anon,   *intends to leave*
And in his compaignye moot I goon.   *must*
Grete wel oure dame, myn owene nece sweete,   *greet*
And fare wel, deere cosyn, til we meete!'   *meet (again)*
365   This marchant, which that was ful war   *cautious; prudent*
         and wys,
Creanced hath, and payd eek in Parys   *obtained credit*
To certeyn Lumbardes, redy in hir hond,
The somme of gold, and gat of hem his bond;

334 A certain number of francs; and some (francs) he took with him.
339 But to ask and see about his welfare.
342 Sir John receives him warmly and entertains him well.
343 And he (the merchant), in return, makes a point of telling him.
345 Thanks be to God, the whole of his merchandise.
347 Raise a loan in his own best interests.
351 As I hope for (eternal) bliss.
354 As well as I am able.
358–9 (And put it back) on your counting-house table; she knows all about it
     by reason of certain vouchers I gave her.
367 *Lumbardes*, Lombards, the moneylenders of medieval Europe.
368 i.e. he recovered his bond for the money he had borrowed.

	And hoom he gooth, murie as a papejay,	*popinjay*
370	For wel he knew he stood in swich array	
	That nedes moste he wynne in that viage	
	A thousand frankes aboven al his costage.	*expenses*
	His wyf ful redy mette hym atte gate,	
	As she was wont of oold usage algate,	
375	And al that nyght in myrthe they bisette;	
	For he was riche and cleerly out of dette.	*completely*
	Whan it was day, this marchant gan embrace	
	His wyf al newe, and kiste hire on hir face,	*all over again*
	And up he gooth and maketh it ful tough.	
380	'Namoore,' quod she, 'by God, ye have ynough!'	
	And wantownly agayn with hym she pleyde,	
	Til atte laste thus this marchant seyde:	
	'By God,' quod he, 'I am a litel wrooth	*angry*
	With yow my wyf, although it be me looth.	*unwilling though I am*
385	And woot ye why? by God, as that I gesse	
	That ye han maad a manere straungenesse	
	Bitwixen me and my cosyn daun John.	
	Ye sholde han warned me, er I had gon,	
	That he yow hadde an hundred frankes payed	
390	By redy token; and heeld hym yvele apayed,	
	For that I to hym spak of chevyssaunce;	*borrowing money*
	Me semed so, as by his contenaunce.	
	But nathelees, by God, oure hevene kyng,	
	I thoughte nat to axen hym no thyng.	
395	I prey thee, wyf, ne do namoore so;	
	Telle me alwey, er that I fro thee go,	
	If any dettour hath in myn absence	*debtor*
	Ypayed thee, lest thurgh thy necligence	
	I myghte hym axe a thing that he hath payed.'	*ask for*
400	This wyf was nat afered nor affrayed,	*frightened; dismayed*
	But boldely she seyde, and that anon:	
	'Marie, I deffie the false monk, daun John!	*marry; defy*
	I kepe nat of his tokenes never a deel;	
	He took me certeyn gold, that woot I weel,—	*gave; know*

370–1 He was so placed that he was sure to make money out of that business trip.
374 As she had long been in the habit of doing.
375 And they spent all that night in jollification.
379 And has an energetic time of it.
385–6 Because I have an idea you caused some unfriendliness.
390 And he was not very pleased.
392 So it seemed to me, by the look on his face.
394 I had no intention of asking him for anything.
395 Don't ever do it again.
403 I care nothing for his vouchers.

405	What! yvel thedam on his monkes snowte!	
	For, God it woot, I wende, withouten doute,	*supposed*
	That he hadde yeve it me bycause of yow,	*given*
	To doon therwith myn honour and my prow,	*benefit*
	For cosynage, and eek for beele cheere	*kinship; hospitality*
410	That he hath had ful ofte tymes heere.	
	But sith I se I stonde in this disjoynt,	*difficult position*
	I wol answere yow shortly to the poynt.	
	Ye han mo slakkere dettours than am I!	*slacker*
	For I wol paye yow wel and redily	
415	Fro day to day, and if so be I faille,	
	I am youre wyf; score it upon my taille,	
	And I shal paye as soone as ever I may.	
	For by my trouthe, I have on myn array,	*clothes*
	And nat on wast, bistowed every deel;	*bit*
420	And for I have bistowed it so weel	
	For youre honour, for Goddes sake, I seye,	
	As be nat wrooth, but lat us laughe and pleye.	
	Ye shal my joly body have to wedde;	*as a pledge*
	By God, I wol nat paye yow but abedde!	*except in bed*
425	Forgyve it me, myn owene spouse deere;	
	Turne hiderward, and maketh bettre cheere.'	
	This marchant saugh ther was no remedie,	*saw*
	And for to chide it nere but folie,	
	Sith that the thyng may nat amended be.	
430	'Now wyf,' he seyde, 'and I foryeve it thee;	
	But, by thy lyf, ne be namoore so large.	*extravagant*
	Keep bet thy good, this yeve I thee in charge.'	
	Thus endeth my tale, and God us sende	
	Taillynge ynough unto oure lyves ende. Amen.	

Heere endeth the Shipmannes Tale

*   *   *   *

405 Bad luck to his monkish snout!
416 Score it on my tally, i.e. charge it to my account.
426 Turn this way, and cheer up.
428 And that it would be silly to scold her.
432 Take better care of my money, I implore you.
434 *Taillynge*, tallying. Both here and in 416 a comic pun is no doubt intended on *taille*, 'tally,' and *tail*, 'tail' (see *Oxford English Dictionary*, *sub*. Tail, *sb.*[1], sense 5c).

The Nun's Priest's Tale

Heere bigynneth the Nonnes Preestes Tale of the Cok and Hen, Chauntecleer and Pertelote

	A POVRE wydwe, somdeel stape in age	*somewhat advanced*
	Was whilom dwellyng in a narwe cotage,	*once; small*
3620	Biside a grove, stondynge in a dale.	
	This wydwe, of which I telle yow my tale,	
	Syn thilke day that she was last a wyf,	*that (same)*
	In pacience ladde a ful symple lyf,	
	For litel was hir catel and hir rente.	*property; income*
3625	By housbondrie of swich as God hire sente	*economical use*
	She foond hirself and eek hir doghtren two.	
	Thre large sowes hadde she, and namo,	*no more*
	Thre keen, and eek a sheep that highte Malle.	
	Ful sooty was hire bour and eek hir halle,	*bower*
3630	In which she eet ful many a sklendre meel.	*slender*
	Of poynaunt sauce hir neded never a deel.	
	No deyntee morsel passed thurgh hir throte;	
	Hir diete was accordant to hir cote.	*in keeping with; cottage*
	Repleccioun ne made hire nevere sik;	*over-eating*
3635	Attempree diete was al hir phisik,	*moderate*
	And exercise, and hertes suffisaunce.	*contentment*
	The goute lette hire nothyng for to daunce,	
	N'apoplexie shente nat hir heed.	*injured*
	No wyn ne drank she, neither whit ne reed;	
3640	Hir bord was served moost with whit and blak, –	
	Milk and broun breed, in which she foond no lak, –	*fault*
	Seynd bacoun, and somtyme an ey or tweye;	*broiled; egg*
	For she was, as it were, a maner deye.	*sort of dairy woman*
	A yeerd she hadde, enclosed al aboute	
3645	With stikkes, and a drye dych withoute,	*stakes*
	In which she hadde a cok, hight Chaunte-	*(who) was called*
	cleer.	
	In al the land, of crowyng nas his peer.	
	His voys was murier than the murie orgon	*pleasanter*
	On messe-dayes that in the chirche gon.	

3626 She provided for herself and her two daughters as well.
3628 Three cows, and also a sheep that was called Moll.
3629 The widow's two-roomed cottage is described in terms of a great house,
with its large public hall and its private room or 'bower' for the lord and lady.
A mock-heroic style is frequently used elsewhere in this poem, as for example
in the description of Chauntecleer, 3656 ff., or in the allusion to the fall of
Troy, 4152 ff.
3631 She had no need of sharp-flavoured sauces.
3637 The gout did not stop her dancing at all.
3647 In all the land there was none his equal in crowing.
3649 That plays in church on feast-days.

3650	Wel sikerer was his crowyng in his logge	
	Than is a clokke or an abbey orlogge.	*clock*
	By nature he knew ech ascencioun	
	Of the equynoxial in thilke toun;	
	For whan degrees fiftene weren ascended,	
3655	Thanne crew he, that it myghte nat been	
	amended.	*bettered*
	His coomb was redder than the fyn coral,	*comb*
	And batailled as it were a castel wal;	*crenellated*
	His byle was blak, and as the jeet it shoon;	*jet*
	Lyk asure were his legges and his toon;	*toes*
3660	His nayles whitter than the lylye flour,	
	And lyk the burned gold was his colour.	*burnished*
	This gentil cok hadde in his governaunce	*noble; control*
	Sevene hennes for to doon al his plesaunce,	*pleasure*
	Whiche were his sustres and his paramours,	*concubines*
3665	And wonder lyk to hym, as of colours;	*wonderfully; in colour*
	Of whiche the faireste hewed on hir throte	
	Was cleped faire damoysele Pertelote.	*called; mistress*
	Curteys she was, discreet, and debonaire,	
	And compaignable, and bar hyrself so faire,	
3670	Syn thilke day that she was seven nyght oold,	*since*
	That trewely she hath the herte in hoold	
	Of Chauntecleer, loken in every lith;	
	He loved hire so that wel was hym therwith.	
	But swich a joye was it to here hem synge,	*such*
3675	Whan that the brighte sonne gan to sprynge,	*rose*
	In sweete accord, 'My lief is faren in londe!'	
	For thilke tyme, as I have understonde,	
	Beestes and briddes koude speke and synge.	
	And so bifel that in a dawenynge,	*dawn*
3680	As Chauntecleer among his wyves alle	
	Sat on his perche, that was in the halle,	
	And next hym sat this faire Pertelote,	
	This Chauntecleer gan gronen in his throte,	*groaned*
	As man that in his dreem is drecched soore.	*troubled*
3685	And whan that Pertelote thus herde hym roore,	*roar*
	She was agast, and seyde, 'Herte deere,	*frightened*
	What eyleth yow, to grone in this manere?	*ails*

3650 The crowing heard in his abode was much more trustworthy.
3652–3 By instinct he could measure, the movement of the equinoctial circle above the horizon in that village.
3666 Of whom the one with the brightest feathers on her throat.
3668–9 She was courteous, discreet, gracious, and friendly, and had behaved so well.
3671–2 That truly she has complete possession of Chauntecleer's heart; *loken in every lith* means literally 'locked in every limb.'
3673 He loved her so much that it made him very happy.
3676 In sweet harmony, 'My love has gone away.'

Ye been a verray sleper; fy, for shame!'   *fine*
  And he answerde, and seyde thus: 'Madame,
3690 I pray yow that ye take it nat agrief.
By God, me mette I was in swich meschief   *I dreamt; trouble*
Right now, that yet myn herte is soore afright.
Now God,' quod he, 'my swevene recche aright
And kepe my body out of foul prisoun!
3695 Me mette how that I romed up and doun   *wandered*
Withinne our yeerd, wheer as I saugh a beest   *saw*
Was lyk an hound, and wolde han maad areest   *seized*
Upon my body, and wolde han had me deed.   *killed me*
His colour was bitwixe yelow and reed,
3700 And tipped was his tayl and bothe his eeris
With blak, unlyk the remenant of his heeris;   *rest*
His snowte smal, with glowynge eyen tweye.   *narrow; two*
Yet of his look for feere almoost I deye;   *fear; die*
This caused me my gronyng, doutelees.'
3705   'Avoy!' quod she, 'fy on yow, hertelees!   *fie; coward*
Allas!' quod she, 'for, by that God above,
Now han ye lost myn herte and al my love.
I kan nat love a coward, by my feith!
For certes, what so any womman seith,   *certainly*
3710 We alle desiren, if it myghte bee,
To han housbondes hardy, wise, and free,   *brave; noble*
And secree, and no nygard, ne no fool,   *discreet; miser*
Ne hym that is agast of every tool,   *weapon*
Ne noon avauntour, by that God above!   *boaster*
3715 How dorste ye seyn, for shame, unto youre love
That any thyng myghte make yow aferd?   *afraid*
Have ye no mannes herte, and han a berd?
Allas! and konne ye been agast of swevenys?   *dreams*
Nothyng, God woot, but vanitee in   *knows; futility*
  sweven is.
3720 Swevenes engendren of replecciouns,
And ofte of fume and of complecciouns,
Whan humours been to habundant in a   *abundant*
  wight.   *person*
Certes this dreem, which ye han met to-nyght,   *this night*
Cometh of the greete superfluytee   *excess*
3725 Of youre rede colera, pardee,   *choler*

3690 I beg you not to be offended.
3693 Interpret my dream favourably, i.e. make its outcome favourable.
3705 *Avoy*, an exclamation of reproach.
3720–1 Dreams are produced by over-eating, and often by noxious vapours
  rising from the stomach and by an unbalanced mixture of the humours. (In
  the following verses Pertelote gives an accurate description of the symptoms of
  choler and melancholy and of the method of treating them. For the 'humours'
  see *General Prologue* 420.)

Which causeth folk to dreden in hir dremes
Of arwes, and of fyr with rede lemes,   *flames*
Of rede beestes, that they wol hem byte,
Of contek, and of whelpes, grete and lyte;
3730   Right as the humour of malencolie   *melancholy*
Causeth ful many a man in sleep to crie
For feere of blake beres, or boles blake,   *bears; bulls*
Or elles blake develes wol him take.
Of othere humours koude I telle also
3735   That werken many a man in sleep ful wo;
But I wol passe as lightly as I kan.
     Lo Catoun, which that was so wys a man,
Seyde he nat thus, "Ne do no fors of dremes?"
     Now sire,' quod she, 'whan we flee fro the bemes,
3740   For Goddes love, as taak som laxatyf.
Up peril of my soule and of my lyf,
I conseille yow the beste, I wol nat lye,   *for the best*
That bothe of colere and of malencolye
Ye purge yow; and for ye shal nat tarie,
3745   Though in this toun is noon apothecarie,
I shal myself to herbes techen yow   *direct*
That shul been for youre hele and for youre   *health*
     prow;   *benefit*
And in oure yeerd tho herbes shal I fynde
The whiche han of hire propretee by kynde
3750   To purge yow bynethe and eek above.
Foryet nat this, for Goddes owene love!   *forget*
Ye been ful coleryk of compleccioun;   *temperament*
Ware the sonne in his ascencioun
Ne fynde yow nat repleet of humours hoote.   *full*
3755   And if it do, I dar wel leye a grote,
That ye shul have a fevere terciane,   *tertian*
Or an agu, that may be youre bane.   *death*
A day or two ye shul have digestyves   *must*
Of wormes, er ye take youre laxatyves   *before*
3760   Of lawriol, centaure, and fumetere,
Or elles of ellebor, that groweth there,   *hellebore*

3729   Of strife, and of dogs, big and small.
3733   Or else of black devils who try to seize them.
3735   That cause many a man great distress in his sleep.
3737   *Catoun*, Dionysius Cato. (See *Miller's Tale* 3227.)
3738   Don't attach any importance to dreams.
3740   For the love of God, please take some laxative.
3744   You purge yourself; and so that you shan't delay.
3749–50   Which have naturally the special power to purge you downwards
     and upwards.
3753   Beware lest the sun in its ascension.
3755   I'll wager a groat (fourpenny-bit).
3760   Laurel, centaury, and fumitory.

Of katapuce, or of gaitrys beryis,
Of herbe yve, growyng in oure yeerd, ther mery is;
Pekke hem up right as they growe and ete hem yn.   *peck*
3765 Be myrie, housbonde, for youre fader kyn!
Dredeth no dreem, I kan sey yow namoore.'
          'Madame,' quod he, 'graunt mercy of youre loore.   *advice*
But nathelees, as touchyng daun Catoun,   *as for*
That hath of wysdom swich a greet renoun,
3770 Though that he bad no dremes for to drede,
By God, men may in olde bookes rede   *read*
Of many a man moore of auctorite
Than evere Caton was, so moot I thee,
That al the revers seyn of this sentence,
3775 And han wel founden by experience
That dremes been significaciouns
As wel of joye as of tribulaciouns   *signs*
That folk enduren in this lif present.
Ther nedeth make of this noon argument;
3780 The verray preeve sheweth it in dede.
          Oon of the gretteste auctour that men rede
Seith thus: that whilom two felawes wente   *once; friends*
On pilgrimage, in a ful good entente;
And happed so, they coomen in a toun   *happened*
3785 Wher as ther was swich congregacioun   *where*
Of peple, and eek so streit of herbergage,
That they ne founde as muche as o cotage
In which they bothe myghte ylogged bee.   *put up*
Wherfore they mosten of necessitee,
3790 As for that nyght, departen compaignye;   *part*
And ech of hem gooth to his hostelrye,
And took his loggyng as it wolde falle.   *as chance decided*
That oon of hem was logged in a stalle,   *one*
Fer in a yeerd, with oxen of the plough;   *far down a yard*
3795 That oother man was logged wel ynough,
As was his aventure or his fortune,   *luck; good fortune*
That us governeth alle as in commune.   *in common*
          And so bifel that, longe er it were day,   *before*
This man mette in his bed, ther as he lay,   *dreamt; where*
3800 How that his felawe gan upon hym calle,   *called*
And seyde, "Allas! for in an oxes stalle

3762 Catapuce, or buckthorn berries.
3763 Buck's-horn, growing in a pleasant spot in our garden.
3765 For the honour of your father's family.
3773 As I hope to prosper.
3774 Who express exactly the opposite of this opinion.
3780 Actual experience shows it to be a fact.
3781 'One of the greatest authors' is a reference to either Cicero or Valerius
      Maximus.
3783 In a most devout frame of mind.
3786 And (which) was also so short of accommodation.

This nyght I shal be mordred ther I lye.   *murdered*
Now help me, deere brother, or I dye.
In alle haste com to me!" he sayde.
3805   This man out of his sleep for feere abrayde;   *woke with a start*
But whan that he was wakened of his sleep,
He turned hym, and took of this no keep.   *turned over; notice*
Hym thoughte his dreem nas but a vanitee.
Thus twies in his slepyng dremed hee;
3810   And atte thridde tyme yet his felawe   *again*
Cam, as hym thoughte, and seide, "I am now slawe.   *slain*
Bihoold my bloody woundes depe and wyde!
Arys up erly in the morwe tyde,   *morning*
And at the west gate of the toun," quod he,
3815   "A carte ful of dong ther shaltow se,
In which my body is hid ful prively;   *secretly*
Do thilke carte arresten boldely.
My gold caused my mordre, sooth to sayn."   *to tell the truth*
And tolde hym every point how he was slayn,
3820   With a ful pitous face, pale of hewe.
And truste wel, his dreem he foond ful trewe,
For on the morwe, as soone as it was day,
To his felawes in he took the way;   *inn*
And whan that he cam to this oxes stalle,
3825   After his felawe he bigan to calle.
The hostiler answerede hym anon,
And seyde, "Sire, your felawe is agon.   *gone*
As soone as day he wente out of the toun."
This man gan fallen in suspecioun,   *became suspicious*
3830   Remembrynge on his dremes that he mette,   *dreamt*
And forth he gooth – no lenger wolde he lette –   *delay*
Unto the west gate of the toun, and fond
A dong-carte, wente as it were to donge lond,
That was arrayed in that same wise   *got ready; way*
3835   As ye han herd the dede man devyse.   *describe*
And with an hardy herte he gan to crye   *brave; called for*
Vengeance and justice of this felonye.
"My felawe mordred is this same nyght,
And in this carte he lith gapyng upright.
3840   I crye out on the ministres," quod he,
"That sholden kepe and reulen this citee.   *watch over*
Harrow! allas! heere lith my felawe slayn!"
What sholde I moore unto this tale sayn?   *why*

3808 It seemed to him his dream was nothing but an idle fancy.
3817 Have that cart stopped boldly.
3833 (Which) went as if to manure the land.
3839 He lies on his back with gaping mouth.
3840 I call on the magistrates.
3842 *Harrow*, a cry for help.

The peple out sterte and caste the cart to grounde,
3845 And in the myddel of the dong they founde
The dede man, that mordred was al newe. *newly*
    O blisful God, that art so just and trewe, *blessed*
Lo, how that thou biwreyest mordre alway! *reveal; always*
Mordre wol out, that se we day by day.
3850 Mordre is so wlatsom and abhomynable
To God, that is so just and resonable,
That he ne wol nat suffre it heled be, *concealed*
Though it abyde a yeer, or two, or thre.
Mordre wol out, this my conclusioun. *this (is)*
3855 And right anon, ministres of that toun
Han hent the carter and so soore hym pyned, *tortured*
And eek the hostiler so soore engyned, *racked*
That they biknewe hire wikkednesse anon, *confessed*
And were anhanged by the nekke-bon. *hanged*
3860   Heere may men seen that dremes been *are*
     to drede. *to be feared*
And certes in the same book I rede,
Right in the nexte chapitre after this –
I gabbe nat, so have I joye or blis –
Two men that wolde han passed over see,
3865 For certeyn cause, into a fer contree,
If that the wynd ne hadde been contrarie,
That made hem in a citee for to tarie
That stood ful myrie upon an haven-syde;
But on a day, agayn the even-tyde,
3870 The wynd gan chaunge, and blew right as hem leste.
Jolif and glad they wente unto hir reste, *cheerful*
And casten hem ful erly for to saille. *resolved*
But herkneth! To that o man fil a greet mervaille:
That oon of hem, in slepyng as he lay,
3875 Hym mette a wonder dreem agayn the day.
Hym thoughte a man stood by his beddes *it seemed to him*
    syde,
And hym comanded that he sholde abyde,
And seyde hym thus: "If thou tomorwe wende,
Thow shalt be dreynt; my tale is at an ende." *drowned*
3880 He wook, and tolde his felawe what he mette,
And preyde hym his viage for to lette;

3850 Murder is so heinous and unnatural.
3863 I do not lie, as I hope for happiness.
3868 That was pleasantly situated on the shore of a haven.
3869–70 But one day, towards evening, the wind changed and blew just as
    they wished.
3873–5 But to one of them a marvellous thing happened: as he lay sleeping he
    dreamt a strange dream just before dawn.
3881 And begged him to postpone his voyage.

As for that day, he preyde hym to byde.   *wait*
His felawe, that lay by his beddes syde,
Gan for to laughe, and scorned him ful faste.
3885   "No dreem," quod he, "may so myn herte agaste   *terrify*
That I wol lette for to do my thynges.
I sette nat a straw by thy dremynges,
For swevenes been but vanytees and japes.
Men dreme alday of owles and of apes,   *constantly*
3890   And of many a maze therwithal;   *delusive thing*
Men dreme of thyng that nevere was ne shal.   *shall (be)*
But sith I see that thou wolt heere abyde,   *since*
And thus forslewthen wilfully thy tyde,
God woot, it reweth me; and have good day!"
3895   And thus he took his leve, and wente his way.
But er that he hadde half his cours yseyled,   *voyage*
Noot I nat why, ne what myschaunce it eyled,
But casuelly the shippes botme rente,
And ship and man under the water wente
3900   In sighte of othere shippes it bisyde,
That with hem seyled at the same tyde.   *time*
And therfore, faire Pertelote so deere,
By swiche ensamples olde maistow leere
That no man sholde been to recchelees   *disregardful*
3905   Of dremes; for I seye thee, doutelees,
That many a dreem ful soore is   *is greatly*
                for to drede.   *to be feared*
   Lo, in the lyf of Seint Kenelm I rede,
That was Kenulphus sone, the noble kyng
Of Mercenrike, how Kenelm mette a thyng.   *Mercia*
3910   A lite er he was mordred, on a day,   *short time before*
His mordre in his avysioun he say.   *vision; saw*
His norice hym expowned every deel
His sweven, and bad hym for to kepe hym weel
For traisoun; but he nas but seven yeer oold,
3915   And therfore litel tale hath he toold   *he took little account*
Of any dreem, so hooly was his herte.
By God! I hadde levere than my sherte   *rather*

3884 Laughed and poured scorn on him.
3886 That I will delay doing my business.
3887–8 I don't care a straw for your dreaming, for dreams are nothing but
    tricks and idle fancies.
3893 And so wilfully waste your time in idleness.
3894 God knows, I'm sorry for it, and so farewell.
3897 I don't know why, nor what went wrong.
3898 By some mischance the ship's bottom was torn open.
3903 From such old stories you may learn.
3912–14 His nurse expounded his dream to him in detail, and begged him to
    guard himself well for fear of treason.
3917–18 i.e. I'd give my shirt to know that you had read the story of his life.

That ye hadde rad his legende, as have I.   *read*
    Dame Pertelote, I sey yow trewely,
3920 Macrobeus, that writ the avisioun
In Affrike of the worthy Cipioun,   *Africa; Scipio*
Affermeth dremes, and seith that they been
Warnynge of thynges that men after seen.   *afterwards*
And forthermoore, I pray yow, looketh wel
3925 In the olde testament, of Daniel,   *concerning*
If he heeld dremes any vanitee.   *idle fancy*
Reed eek of Joseph, and ther shul ye see   *also*
Wher dremes be somtyme – I sey nat alle –   *whether*
Warnynge of thynges that shul after falle.   *happen*
3930 Looke of Egipte the kyng, daun Pharao,
His bakere and his butiller also,   *butler*
Wher they ne felte noon effect in dremes.
Whoso wol seken actes of sondry remes
May rede of dremes many a wonder thyng.
3935 Lo Cresus, which that was of Lyde kyng,   *Croesus; Lydia*
Mette he nat that he sat upon a tree,   *not*
Which signified he sholde anhanged bee?
Lo heere Andromacha, Ectores wyf,   *Andromache*
That day that Ector sholde lese his lyf,   *was to lose*
3940 She dremed on the same nyght biforn
How that the lyf of Ector sholde be lorn,   *would be lost*
If thilke day he wente into bataille.   *that*
She warned hym, but it myghte nat availle;
He wente for to fighte natheles,   *nevertheless*
3945 But he was slayn anon of Achilles.
But thilke tale is al to longe to telle,
And eek it is ny day, I may nat dwelle.   *near*
Shortly I seye, as for conclusioun,
That I shal han of this avisioun   *have from*
3950 Adversitee; and I seye forthermoor,
That I ne telle of laxatyves no stoor,
For they been venymes, I woot it weel;
I hem diffye, I love hem never a deel!
    Now let us speke of myrthe, and stynte al this.   *stop*
3955 Madame Pertelote, so have I blis,
Of o thyng God hath sent me large grace;
For whan I se the beautee of youre face,

3920 Macrobius was the author of a commentary (*c.* AD 400) on Cicero's
    Somnium Scipionis.
3925 Dan. vii ff.
3930 Consider the king of Egypt, lord Pharaoh (Gen. xl, xli).
3932 Whether they felt no consequences of dreams.
3933 Anyone who will search the histories of various realms.
3951 That I set no store by laxatives.
3953 I spurn them – I don't like them a bit!
3956 In one thing God has sent me great good fortune.

Ye been so scarlet reed aboute youre yen,   *eyes*
It maketh al my drede for to dyen;
3960 For al so siker as *In principio*,
Mulier est hominis confusio, –
Madame, the sentence of this Latyn is,   *meaning*
"Womman is mannes joye and al his blis."
For whan I feele a-nyght your softe syde,   *at night*
3965 Al be it that I may nat on yow ryde,
For that oure perche is maad so narwe, allas!   *narrow*
I am so ful of joye and of solas,   *delight*
That I diffye bothe sweven and dreem.'
And with that word he fley doun fro the beem,   *flew*
3970 For it was day, and eke his hennes alle,
And with a chuk he gan hem for to calle,   *cluck*
For he hadde founde a corn, lay in the yerd.
Real he was, he was namoore aferd.   *regal*
He fethered Pertelote twenty tyme,
3975 And trad hire eke as ofte, er it was pryme.
He looketh as it were a grym leoun,   *like a fierce lion*
And on his toos he rometh up and doun;   *stalks*
Hym deigned nat to sette his foot to grounde.   *he did not deign*
He chukketh whan he hath a corn yfounde,
3980 And to hym rennen thanne his wyves alle.
Thus roial, as a prince is in his halle,
Leve I this Chauntecleer in his pasture,
And after wol I telle his aventure.
      Whan that the month in which the world bigan,
3985 That highte March, whan God first maked man,   *is called*
Was compleet, and passed were also,
Syn March was gon, thritty dayes and two,
Bifel that Chauntecleer in al his pryde,
His sevene wyves walkynge by his syde,
3990 Caste up his eyen to the brighte sonne,
That in the signe of Taurus hadde yronne
Twenty degrees and oon, and somwhat moore,
And knew by kynde, and by noon oother   *instinct*
      loore,   *learning*

3959 It makes all my fear die away.
3960–1 For it's as true as the gospel (*In principio* are the opening words of St
    John's Gospel) that 'Woman is man's ruin.' See *General Prologue* 254.
3968 I defy both vision and dream.
3972 A grain of corn which lay in the yard.
3975 *pryme*, first division of the day (6–9 a.m.). Here and in 3994 the later
    hour of 9 a.m. is meant.
3982 I leave Chauntecleer feeding.
3984–7 A roundabout way of saying 'When it was May 3rd.' *Syn March bigan*
    may be understood as meaning 'since March began (and ended).'
3990–2 i.e. the sun in its annual course (according to the Ptolemaic system of
    astronomy) was in the 22nd degree of the zodiacal sign Taurus; this again
    points to May 3rd.

That it was pryme, and crew with blisful stevene.   *voice*
3995 'The sonne,' he seyde, 'is clomben up on hevene   *climbed*
Fourty degrees and oon, and moore ywis.
Madame Pertelote, my worldes blis,
Herkneth thise blisful briddes how they synge,
And se the fresshe floures how they sprynge;   *grow*
4000 Ful is myn herte of revel and solas!'   *joy*
But sodeynly hym fil a sorweful cas,   *mischance*
For evere the latter ende of joye is wo.
God woot that worldly joye is soone ago;   *gone*
And if a rethor koude faire endite,
4005 He in a cronycle saufly myghte it write
As for a sovereyn notabilitee.
Now every wys man, lat him herkne me:
This storie is also trewe, I undertake,
As is the book of Launcelot de Lake,
4010 That wommen holde in ful greet reverence.   *whom*
Now wol I torne agayn to my sentence.   *subject*
A col-fox, ful of sly iniquitee,
That in the grove hadde woned yeres three,
By heigh ymaginacioun forncast,
4015 The same nyght thurghout the hegges brast   *burst*
Into the yerd ther Chauntecleer the faire
Was wont, and eek his wyves, to repaire;
And in a bed of wortes still he lay,   *cabbages*
Til it was passed undren of the day,   *noon*
4020 Waitynge his tyme on Chauntecleer   *watching his opportunity*
    to falle,
As gladly doon thise homycides alle
That in await liggen to mordre men.
O false mordrour, lurkynge in thy den!
O newe Scariot, newe Genylon,
4025 False dissymulour, o Greek Synon,   *dissembler*
That broghtest Troye al outrely to sorwe!   *utterly*
O Chauntecleer, acursed be that morwe

3995–6 The sun's altitude at 9 a.m. on May 3rd is correctly given by
    Chauntecleer as rather more than 41°.
4002 For joy always ends in sorrow.
4004–6 And if a master of rhetoric knew his job, he could confidently write it
    down in a chronicle as a most notable fact.
4008 This story is as true, I give you my word.
4009 An allusion to the story of Lancelot, the lover of Queen Guinevere.
4012 *col-fox*, 'coal fox,' i.e. fox with black markings.
4014 As foreseen by divine foreknowledge.
4021–2 As all assassins usually do that lie in wait to murder men.
4024 *Scariot*, Judas Iscariot: *Genylon*, Ganelon, the man who betrays Roland in
    the *Chanson de Roland*.
4025 *Synon*, Sinon, the Greek who persuaded the Trojans to receive the wooden
    horse into Troy.

That thou into that yerd flaugh fro the bemes!   *flew*
Thou were ful wel ywarned by thy dremes
4030   That thilke day was perilous to thee;
But what that God forwoot moot nedes bee,
After the opinioun of certein clerkis.   *according; scholars*
Witnesse on hym that any parfit clerk is,
That in scole is greet altercacioun
4035   In this mateere, and greet disputisoun,   *debate*
And hath been of an hundred thousand men.
But I ne kan nat bulte it to the bren,
As kan the hooly doctour Augustyn,
Or Boece, or the Bisshop Bradwardyn,
4040   Wheither that Goddes worthy forwityng   *foreknowledge*
Streyneth me nedely for to doon a   *constrains; necessarily*
             thyng, –
'Nedely' clepe I symple necessitee;   *call*
Or elles, if free choys be graunted me
To do that same thyng, or do it noght,   *not*
4045   Though God forwoot it er that I was wroght;
Or if his wityng streyneth never a deel
But by necessitee condicioneel.
I wol nat han to do of swich mateere;
My tale is of a cok, as ye may heere,
4050   That tok his conseil of his wyf, with sorwe,
To walken in the yerd upon that morwe
That he hadde met that dreem that I yow tolde.
Wommennes conseils been ful ofte colde;   *very often fatal*
Wommannes conseil broghte us first to wo,
4055   And made Adam fro Paradys to go,
Ther as he was ful myrie and wel at ese.
But for I noot to whom it myght displese,   *know not*
If I conseil of wommen wolde blame,
Passe over, for I seyde it in my game.   *in fun*
4060   Rede auctours, where they trete of swich mateere,
And what they seyn of wommen ye may heere.

4031 But whatever God foreknows must necessarily be.
4033–4 Take any accomplished scholar as witness that in the schools (i.e.
    universities).
4037 But I cannot sift the flour from the bran, i.e. find out the truth of the
    matter.
4038–9 *Augustyn*, St Augustine of Hippo (345–430); *Boece* Boethius (*d.* 524),
    author of *De Consolatione Philosophiae*, which Chaucer translated; *Bradwardyn*,
    Thomas Bradwardine, Archbishop of Canterbury (*d.* 1349). These three are
    named here as authorities on the problem of the relationship between free will
    and predestination.
4045 Though God foreknows it before I was born.
4046–7 Or if His knowledge involves no constraint at all, except that of
    conditional necessity (i.e. the necessity implied by divine foreknowledge that a
    thing will come to pass).
4050 Who took his wife's advice – bad luck to him!
4056 Where he was very happy and comfortable.

Thise been the cokkes wordes, and nat myne;
I kan noon harm of no womman divyne.
    Faire in the soond, to bathe hire myrily,
4065 Lith Pertelote, and alle hire sustres by,
Agayn the sonne, and Chauntecleer so free   *noble*
Soong murier than the mermayde in the see;   *more sweetly*
For Phisiologus seith sikerly   *truly*
How that they syngen wel and myrily.
4070 And so bifel that, as he caste his ye
Among the wortes on a boterflye,
He was war of this fox, that lay ful lowe.
Nothyng ne liste hym thanne for to crowe,
But cride anon, 'Cok! cok!' and up he sterte
4075 As man that was affrayed in his herte.
For natureelly a beest desireth flee
Fro his contrarie, if he may it see,
Though he never erst hadde seyn it with his ye.   *previously*
    This Chauntecleer, whan he gan hym   *caught sight of him*
        espye,
4080 He wolde han fled, but that the fox anon
Seyde, 'Gentil sire, allas! wher wol ye gon?
Be ye affrayed of me that am youre freend?
Now, certes, I were worse than a feend,
If I to yow wolde harm or vileynye!   *intended; bad turn*
4085 I am nat come youre conseil for t'espye,   *secrets; spy out*
But trewely, the cause of my comynge
Was oonly for to herkne how that ye synge.
For trewely, ye have as myrie a stevene
As any aungel hath that is in hevene.
4090 Therwith ye han in musyk moore feelynge
Than hadde Boece, or any that kan synge.
My lord youre fader – God his soule blesse!—
And eek youre mooder, of hire gentillesse,
Han in myn hous ybeen to my greet ese;
4095 And certes, sire, ful fayn wolde I yow plese.
But, for men speke of syngyng, I wol seye, –
So moote I brouke wel myne eyen tweye, –

4063 I can think no harm of any woman.
4064–6 Pertelote, with all her sisters beside her, lies elegantly in the sand and
    there, in the sunshine, takes a pleasant bath.
4068 *Phisiologus*, the medieval Latin bestiary or book of beasts, in which the
    song of the Sirens (identified with mermaids in Chaucer's tale) is interpreted as
    a symbol of deceitful worldly pleasure.
4073 Then he had no desire at all to crow.
4091 Boethius wrote a treatise on music which was a standard text-book in the
    Middle Ages.
4093–4 (They) did me the courtesy of visiting me in my house, to my great
    satisfaction.
4097 As I hope to make good use of my two eyes.

Save yow, I herde nevere man so synge   *except for*
As dide youre fader in the morwenynge.
4100 Certes, it was of herte, al that he song.   *from the heart*
And for to make his voys the moore strong,
He wolde so peyne hym that with bothe his yen
He moste wynke, so loude he wolde cryen,
And stonden on his tiptoon therwithal,   *tiptoes*
4105 And strecche forth his nekke long and smal.   *slender*
And eek he was of swich discrecioun   *discernment*
That ther nas no man in no regioun
That hym in song or wisedom myghte passe.   *surpass*
I have wel rad in "Daun Burnel the Asse,"
4110 Among his vers, how that ther was a cok,
For that a preestes sone yaf hym a knok   *because*
Upon his leg whil he was yong and nyce,
He made hym for to lese his benefice.   *lose*
But certeyn, ther nys no comparisoun
4115 Bitwixe the wisedom and discrecioun
Of youre fader and of his subtiltee.
Now syngeth, sire, for seinte charitee;   *holy*
Lat se, konne ye youre fader countrefete?'
This Chauntecleer his wynges gan to bete,
4120 As man that koude his traysoun nat espie,   *one*
So was he ravysshed with his flaterie.
Allas! ye lordes, many a fals flatour   *flatterer*
Is in youre courtes, and many a losengeour,   *deceiver*
That plesen yow wel moore, by my feith,   *much*
4125 Than he that soothfastnesse unto yow seith.   *truth*
Redeth Ecclesiaste of flaterye;
Beth war, ye lordes, of hir trecherye.
This Chauntecleer stood hye upon his toos,
Strecchynge his nekke, and heeld his eyen cloos,
4130 And gan to crowe loude for the nones.   *for the occasion*
And daun Russell the fox stirte up atones,
And by the gargat hente Chauntecleer,   *throat; seized*
And on his bak toward the wode hym beer,   *carried*
For yet ne was ther no man that hym sewed.   *pursued*
4135 O destinee, that mayst nat been eschewed!   *avoided*
Allas, that Chauntecleer fleigh fro the bemes!   *flew*

4102–3 He would exert himself so much that he had to close both his eyes.
4109 I have read indeed in 'Lord Burnel the Ass.' (A donkey named Burnellus is
     the hero of a Latin satirical poem on the regular clergy written by Nigel
     Wireker, a twelfth-century monk of Christ Church, Canterbury.)
4112 While he (i.e. the priest's son) was young and foolish.
4116 And his (i.e. that cock's) ingenuity.
4118 Show me whether you can imitate your father.
4126 Ecclus. xxvii. 26; Prov. xxix. 5.

Allas, his wyf ne roghte nat of dremes!
And on a Friday fil al this meschaunce.   *misfortune*
  O Venus, that art goddesse of plesaunce,   *pleasure*
4140 Syn that thy servant was this Chauntecleer,
And in thy servyce dide al his poweer,   *did his utmost*
Moore for delit than world to multiplye,   *delight*
Why woldestow suffre hym on thy day to dye?
  O Gaufred, deere maister soverayn,
4145 That whan thy worthy kyng Richard was slayn
With shot, compleynedest his deeth so soore,
Why ne hadde I now thy sentence and thy loore,
The Friday for to chide, as diden ye?
For on a Friday, soothly, slayn was he.
4150 Thanne wolde I shewe yow how that I koude
    pleyne
For Chauntecleres drede and for his peyne.   *fear; suffering*
  Certes, swich cry ne lamentacion,
Was nevere of ladyes maad whan Ylion   *Ilion*
Was wonne, and Pirrus with his streite swerd,
4155 Whan he hadde hent kyng Priam by the berd,
And slayn hym, as seith us *Eneydos*,
As maden alle the hennes in the clos,   *yard*
Whan they had seyn of Chauntecleer the sighte.
But sovereynly dame Pertelote shrighte,
4160 Ful louder than dide Hasdrubales wyf,
Whan that hir housbonde hadde lost his lyf,
And that the Romayns hadde brend Cartage.   *burnt*
She was so ful of torment and of rage   *anguish; frenzy*
That wilfully into the fyr she sterte,   *deliberately; leapt*
4165 And brende hirselven with a stedefast herte.
  O woful hennes, right so criden ye,
As, whan that Nero brende the citee
Of Rome, cryden senatoures wyves
For that hir husbondes losten alle hir lyves, –
4170 Withouten gilt this Nero hath hem slayn.
Now wole I turne to my tale agayn.

4137 Alas, that his wife took no heed of dreams.
4144 *Gaufred*, Geoffrey de Vinsauf, whose *Poetria Nova*, an early thirteenth-
    century treatise on the art of poetry, had considerable influence on Chaucer as
    a young poet. The maturer Chaucer, as the irony of this allusion shows, had
    outgrown Geoffrey's precepts and models.
4145 Richard I (*d.* 1199).
4146 By the shooting of an arrow, lamented his death so bitterly.
4147 Why haven't I now your noble sentiments and learning.
4154–5 And when Pyrrhus with his drawn sword had seized King Priam.
4156 *Aeneid*, ii. 550 ff.
4159 But madam Pertelote shrieked above all the others.
4160 Hasdrubal was the king of Carthage when the Romans burnt it in 146 B.C.

This sely wydwe and eek hir doghtres two   *poor*
Herden thise hennes crie and maken wo,   *lamentation*
And out at dores stirten they anon,   *rushed*
4175 And syen the fox toward the grove gon,   *saw*
And bar upon his bak the cok away,
And cryden, 'Out! harrow! and weylaway!   *alas*
Ha! ha! the fox!' and after hym they ran,
And eek with staves many another man.
4180 Ran Colle oure dogge, and Talbot, and Gerland,
And Malkyn, with a dystaf in hir hand;
Ran cow and calf, and eek the verray hogges,
So fered for the berkyng of the dogges   *frightened because of*
And shoutyng of the men and wommen eeke,
4185 They ronne so hem thoughte hir herte breeke.
They yolleden as feendes doon in helle;   *yelled*
The dokes cryden as men wolde hem quelle;   *ducks; kill*
The gees for feere flowen over the trees;
Out of the hyve cam the swarm of bees.
4190 So hydous was the noyse, a, *benedicitee*!   *hideous; bless us*
Certes, he Jakke Straw and his meynee
Ne made nevere shoutes half so shrille
Whan that they wolden any Flemyng kille,
As thilke day was maad upon the fox.
4195 Of bras they broghten bemes, and of box,   *trumpets; boxwood*
Of horn, of boon, in whiche they blewe and   *bone*
   powped,   *tooted*
And therwithal they skriked and they   *shrieked*
   howped.   *whooped*
It semed as that hevene sholde falle.
   Now, goode men, I prey yow herkneth alle:
4200 Lo, how Fortune turneth sodeynly   *overturns*
The hope and pryde eek of hir enemy!
This cok, that lay upon the foxes bak,
In al his drede unto the fox he spak,
And seyde, 'Sire, if that I were as ye,
4205 Yet sholde I seyn, as wys God helpe me,
"Turneth agayn, ye proude cherles alle!   *back; churls*
A verray pestilence upon yow falle!
Now I am come unto the wodes syde;
Maugree youre heed, the cok shal heere abyde.

4180 *Talbot* and *Gerland* are dogs' names.
4181 *Malkyn*, diminutive of *Moll*.
4185 They ran so hard it seemed to them their hearts would break.
4191 Surely Jack Straw and his following. (Jack Straw was one of the leaders of the Peasants' Revolt in 1381. The massacre of the Flemings by the London mob was due to envy of their success as woollen merchants and manufacturers.)
4204–5 If I were you . . . so help me God.
4209 In spite of all you can do (lit. in spite of your head), the cock shall stay here.

4210 I wol hym ete, in feith, and that anon!" '   *immediately*
    The fox answerde, 'In feith, it shal be don.'
And as he spak that word, al sodeynly
This cok brak from his mouth delyverly,
And heighe upon a tree he fleigh anon.
4215 And whan the fox saugh that the cok was gon,
    'Allas!' quod he, 'O Chauntecleer, allas!
I have to yow,' quod he, 'ydoon trespas,   *done wrong*
In as muche as I maked yow aferd
Whan I yow hente and broghte out of the yerd.
4220 But, sire, I dide it in no wikke entente.
Com doun, and I shal telle yow what I mente;
I shal seye sooth to yow, God help me so!'
    'Nay thanne,' quod he, 'I shrewe us bothe two.   *curse*
And first I shrewe myself, bothe blood and bones,
4225 If thou bigyle me ofter than ones.   *fool*
Thou shalt namoore, thurgh thy flaterye,
Do me to synge and wynke with myn ye;
For he that wynketh, whan he sholde see,
Al wilfully, God lat him nevere thee!'   *prosper*
4230   'Nay,' quod the fox, 'but God yeve hym meschaunce,
That is so undiscreet of governaunce
That jangleth whan he sholde holde his pees.'   *chatters*
    Lo, swich it is for to be recchelees
And necligent, and truste on flaterye.
4235   But ye that holden this tale a folye,   *silly thing*
As of a fox, or of a cok and hen,
Taketh the moralite, goode men.
For seint Paul seith that al that writen is,
To oure doctrine it is ywrite, ywis;
4240 Taketh the fruyt, and lat the chaf be stille.
Now, goode God, if that it be thy wille,
As seith my lord, so make us alle goode men,
And brynge us to his heighe blisse! Amen.

Heere is Ended the Nonnes Preestes Tale

4213 Nimbly escaped from his mouth.
4224 I curse myself utterly.
4227 Make me sing and shut my eyes.
4231 So lacking in self-control.
4233 See, this is what happens when you are thoughtless.
4239 Is written for our instruction, certainly. (See Rom. xv. 4.)
4242 *my lord.* A marginal note in the Ellesmere MS. explains this as an allusion
    to the Archbishop of Canterbury; but the point of the allusion is lost.

Epilogue to the Nun's Priest's Tale

'SIRE Nonnes Preest,' oure Hooste seide anoon,
4245 'I-blessed be thy breche, and every stoon!   *breeches*
This was a murie tale of Chauntecleer.
But by my trouthe, if thou were seculer,
Thou woldest ben a trede-foul aright.
For if thou have corage as thou hast myght,   *desire*
4250 Thee were nede of hennes, as I wene,
Ya, moo than seven tymes seventene.   *yea*
See, whiche braunes hath this gentil preest,   *what muscles*
So gret a nekke, and swich a large breest!
He loketh as a sperhauk with his yen;   *sparrow-hawk; eyes*
4255 Him nedeth nat his colour for to dyen
With brasile, ne with greyn of Portyngale.
Now, sire, faire falle yow for youre tale!'   *good luck to you*
    And after that he, with ful merie chere,   *cheerfully*
Seide unto another, as ye shuln heere.

4250 You would have need of hens.
4255–6 He doesn't need to put colour into his face by using red dyes made from
    brazil-wood or cochineal.

Appendices

I. Note on Pronunciation
(Line references are to the *General Prologue*)

SHORT VOWELS

a as in German *Mann*, French *patte*: Whan that 1, March 2.

e (stressed) as in *men*: every 3, vertu 4, tendre 7.

e (unstressed) as in *about*: shoures 1, soote 1, perced 2.

i, y as in *bit*: with 1, inspired 6, knyght 42.

o as in *bog*: croppes 7, holpen 18, on 19.

u (sometimes written *o*) as in *full*: yonge sonne 7, but 35.

LONG VOWELS

a, aa as in *father*: smale 9, maken 9, caas 323.

e, ee, ie (close) as in German *lehnen*, French *été*: sweete 5, slepen 10, coverchiefs 453.

e, ee (open) as in French *père*: were 26, esed 29, nathelees 35.

i, y as in *see*: inspired 6, ye 10, shires 15.

o, oo (close) as in German *Sohn*, French *beau*: soote 1, roote 2, wolden 27.

o, oo (open) as in *saw*: open 10, goon 12, spoken 31.

ou, ow, o(gh) as in *moon*: shoures 1, droghte 2, foweles 9.

u as in French *tu*: vertu 4, nature 11, aventure 25.

DIPHTHONGS

ai, ay, ei, ey approximately a combination of *a* and *i*: veyne 3, day 19, wey 34.

au, aw as in *house*: straunge 13, Caunterbury 16, felaweshipe 32.

eu, ew as in *few*: newe 176, knew 240, trewe 531.

oi, oy as in *boy*: coy 119, Loy 120.

CONSONANTS

Unfamiliar sounds and spellings include:

ch, cch as in *church*: Chivalrie 45, recchelees 179.

g, gg as in *bridge*: corages 11, juggement 818.

gh (after a front vowel) as in German *ich*: nyght 10, knyght 42.

gh (after a back vowel) as in Scots *loch*: droghte 2.

h is silent in French loan-words like *honoured* 50, and weakly pronounced in native words like *he, his, her(e), hem*.

r as trilled *r* in Scots: Aprill 1, shoures 1, droghte 2.

sh, ssh as in *shall*: parisshe 491.

wh as in Scots *white*: which 4, whan 30.

Note: Both consonants should be pronounced in words like *k*new 240, *w*rite 96, ha*l*ve 8, yo*n*ge 7; double consonants should be distinguished from single consonants, e.g. *sonne* (pronounced *sun-ne*) 7 and *sone* (pronounced *su-ne*) 336.

II. Note on Grammar

The following brief note includes some of Chaucer's grammatical forms which may cause difficulty to a modern reader.

1. *Nouns.*

(i) Some nouns have no ending in the genitive singular: *his lady grace*, 'his lady's grace'; *hir doghter name*, 'her daughter's name'; *by my fader kyn*, 'by my father's kin.'

(ii) A few nouns have no ending in the plural: *hors*, 'horses'; *yeer* (beside *yeres*), 'years.'

(iii) A few nouns form their plural in –(*e*)*n*: *eyen*, 'eyes'; *sustren*, 'sisters'; *toon*, 'toes.'

2. *Adjectives.*

(i) The plural ends in –*e*: *olde bokes*, 'old books'; *swiche men*, 'such men.'

(ii) The singular of the weak form of adjectives (used after demonstratives and in the vocative) also ends in –*e*: *the yonge sonne*, 'the young sun'; *O goode God*.

3. *Pronouns.*

(i) *Second Person.* The singular pronouns *thou, thee* are used in familiar talk, in addressing an inferior, or in a prayer to God; the plural pronouns *ye, you* are used in addressing a superior. *Ye* (nominative) is kept distinct from *you* (accusative and dative).

(ii) *Third Person.*

  (*a*) The possessive singular feminine is *hir(e), her(e)*, 'her.'

  (*b*) The possessive singular neuter is *his*, 'its' (nominative *it, hit*).

  (*c*) The plural forms are *they; hir(e), her(e)*, 'their'; *hem*, 'them.'

4. *Relative*.

(i) *That* is the commonest form, and is used for persons as well as things.

(ii) *Which(e)* is also used, frequently preceded by *the* or followed by *that*: *the Erl of Panyk, which that hadde tho Wedded his suster*, 'the Earl of Panyk, who had then married his sister.'

5. *Verbs*.

(i) The present indicative second and third person singular endings are *–(e)st*, *–(e)th*. Contracted forms ending in *–t* are sometimes found in the third person: *bit*, 'bids'; *rist*, 'rises'; *rit*, 'rides'; *sit*, 'sits.'

(ii) The present indicative plural ending is *–(e)n*: *they wende*, 'they go'; *Thanne longen folk*, 'then people long.'

(iii) The imperative plural ends in *–(e)th* or *–e*. A polite imperative is sometimes used, preceded by *as*: *as beth of bettre cheere*, 'please be more cheerful.'

(iv) The past participle often retains the old prefix *y–*: *ybore(n)*, 'born'; *ykept*, 'kept.'

(v) Reflexive and impersonal verbs are both commoner in Chaucer's English than in modern English: *noght avaunte thee*, 'don't boast'; *deliteth hym*, 'he delights'; *me were levere*, 'I would rather'; *hym oghte*, 'he ought.'

(vi) *gan* is often used with an infinitive to form the simple past tense: *oon of hem gan callen to his knave*, 'one of them called out to his servant.'

III. Note on Versification

During the past four hundred years there have been several shifts of opinion about the nature of Chaucer's versification. From the sixteenth to the eighteenth centuries his verse was generally considered to be rhythmical, but not metrically regular. There was some dissent, but most readers would have agreed with Dryden that Chaucer's verse had 'the rude Sweetness of a *Scotch* Tune . . . which is natural and pleasing, though not perfect' (Preface to *Fables Ancient and Modern*, 1700). After the publication in 1775 of Tyrwhitt's *Essay on the Language and Versification of Chaucer* (vol. iv of his edition of *The Canterbury Tales*), the opinion gained ground that Chaucer had made extensive metrical use of inflectional *–e*, and that if this is pronounced where it should be the apparent irregularities of his verse largely disappear. Opinion hardened into dogma during the second half of the nineteenth century with the appearance of F. J. Child's *Observations on the Language of Chaucer* (1861–3) and of a series of editions of *The Canterbury Tales* based on a normalized Ellesmere text (headed by Skeat's great Oxford Chaucer in 1894). But since then the publication of Manly and Rickert's text of *The Canterbury Tales* (1940) has encouraged the belief that the late nineteenth-century editors went too far in the direction of metrical regularity, basing their theories on 'an artificial text made regular by all the devices at the disposal of the scholar' (Manly and Rickert, ii 40–1). J. G. Southworth, in his *Verses of Cadence* (1954), flatly denies that Chaucer pronounced final –e either within the verse or at the end of it, and maintains that he wrote in freely rhythmical verse rather than in iambic foot-units.

These two different ways of reading (and hearing) Chaucer's verse are perhaps not as completely irreconcilable as they seem to be at first glance. A great many of Chaucer's verses can be read quite naturally with an iambic movement if final –e is normally pronounced within the line, but elided before an initial vowel or a weak *h*, and slurred at the end of such words as *youre, hire, whiche, were*:

> A Clérk ther wás of Óxenfórd alsó,
> That únto lógyk háddë lóng(e) ygo. . . .
> Sównyng(e) in móral vértu wás his spéche,
> And gládly wóld(e) he lérn(e) and gládly téche.

Further, it has to be remembered that Chaucer is always varying the regular iambic-decasyllabic pattern, as the rhythms of natural speech dictate. For example, at the beginning of the third verse above the iambic is replaced by a trochaic movement. If we read Chaucer's verse with natural stressing and with due regard for the elision or slurring of final –e, we find that he gives us a strongly rhythmical movement of infinite variety, but one which is disciplined by the basic pattern of iambic verse.

Various recordings of extracts from *The Canterbury Tales*, read by scholars, have been produced. Some of these are marketed commercially, and are also often available from public libraries. Such recordings can help the reader form an impression of how Chaucer's work might have sounded when read aloud.

Everyman's Poetry

Titles available in this series

William Blake
ed. Peter Butter
0 460 87800 X

The Brontës
ed. Pamela Norris
0 460 87864 6

Rupert Brooke & Wilfred Owen
ed. George Walter
0 460 87801 8

Robert Browning
ed. Colin Graham
0 460 87893 X

Robert Burns
ed. Donald Low
0 460 87814 X

Lord Byron
ed. Jane Stabler
0 460 87810 7

Geoffrey Chaucer:
Comic and Bawdy Tales
ed. Malcolm Andrew
0 460 87869 7

John Clare
ed. R. K. R. Thornton
0 460 87823 9

Samuel Taylor Coleridge
ed. John Beer
0 460 87826 3

Emily Dickinson
ed. Helen McNeil
0 460 87895 6

John Donne
ed. D. J. Enright
0 460 87901 4

Four Metaphysical Poets
ed. Douglas Brooks-Davies
0 460 87857 3

Oliver Goldsmith
ed Robert L. Mack
0 460 87827 1

Thomas Gray
ed. Robert L. Mack
0 460 87805 0

Ivor Gurney
ed. George Walter
0 460 87797 6

Heinrich Heine
ed. T. J. Reed & David Cram
0 460 87865 4

George Herbert
ed. D. J. Enright
0 460 87795 X

Robert Herrick
ed. Douglas Brooks-Davies
0 460 87799 2